R O C K

"I could walk out of here and ridicule your parents or curse God and most of you wouldn't do a thing. But if I said one word against your favorite rock group, some of you would tear me limb from limb.

"You see, rock is something more than just a form of music. To teens today it is a way of life that nearly consumes their every waking moment."

Bob Larson knows. He's been an entertainer, he's young, and he's done his research. So whether you're adult or teen, whether you agree with him or not, you must listen to what he says.

ROCK
BOB LARSON

LIVING BOOKS

Tyndale House Publishers, Inc.
Wheaton, Illinois

Readers may write to the
author at the following address:

Bob Larson Ministries
Box 26480
Denver, CO 80236

First printing, Living Books edition, April 1982
Library of Congress Catalog Card Number 79-55755, paper
81-85679, Living Books edition
ISBN 0-8423-5685-1, paper
0-8423-5686-X, Living Books edition
Printed in the United States of America

CONTENTS

ONE
GRILLED PREACHER

I should have known the moment we got into the car that I was
in for it. The teenager driving us to our Sunday luncheon
engagement had tuned the radio to his favorite rock station. It
blared at full volume, the heaviest sounds he could find
on the dial, and the worst was yet to come. We were headed for
his parents' home.

It's not often that I accept private dinner invitations. One reason
is the busy schedule I follow. There is just not enough
time to respond favorably to every offer that graciously comes my
way. Another reason is my waistline. Good physical conditioning
is important to me. There would be little point in jogging
my usual three miles a day and then sitting down to three
sumptuous meals to gorge my appetite.

But I need not have worried about the calories of this particular
meal. The main course on the menu was me. I had been
invited not to eat but to be eaten.

It was a long drive to the house—and a noisy one. Attempting
conversation was pointless. The radio wouldn't permit it.
I sat quietly in the back seat next to my wife. She looked at me with
a questioning gaze that seemed to ask what we were in for.
No one said a word. The air waves were, for the moment, under
the control of the Rolling Stones and Rod Stewart.

Parents know what I was going through. They're used to
enduring or policing their children's music, but this was quite a

shock to my system. Please give me your sympathy. Remember, Kathy and I do not have any children and we do have similar musical tastes. The music in our home and car is what we both like to hear.

I enjoy some popular music myself. After all, before I became a Christian, music was my life. As a professional entertainer I was immersed in the music of my day. I wrote it, sang it, and played it. But that was in the "Happy Days" of white bucks and Fats Domino. Our songs may have been occasionally shady, but we never dreamed of the sadomasochistic fantasies of KISS or the demonic overtones of Black Sabbath.

I still like a song with a good rhythm. As a guitar player, Segovia is not the only style I appreciate. But I do draw the line somewhere. When the lyrics explore the obscene and profane, when the entertainers glorify the perverse and forbidden, and when the beat borders on the erotic, that's where I say, "No!"

I was ready to say it now. After just walking out of the solemnity of a worship service, I wasn't quite prepared to hear my driver's favorite rock group sing of smoking pot and sleeping with groupies. In fact, I probably would have said something if it hadn't been for my wife's elbow in my ribs. Tact and diplomacy were never my best virtues. Maybe it was best for her to "gently" remind me this wasn't our car, and it was none of my business what kind of music my driver was listening to.

Anyway, I knew that, in part, it was being done for my benefit. I had announced that morning that in the evening service I was going to speak on the subject of rock music. Every aspect would be explored in the message: lyrics that present themes of drugs, sex, perversion, and blasphemy, and singers who portray images of sexual licentiousness and drug advocacy.

Maybe I had it coming. Because this teenage son was so used to being harped at for the music he listened to, perhaps he just naturally assumed I had been called in as the spiritual gunslinger for the Establishment. He expected me to try to cram down his throat all the cultural hang-ups of his parents. So, he was going to get to me first.

It was working! Parents, put yourself in my place. How would you like to be locked in your teenager's room for an hour to listen to all of his albums? Here I was in the back seat of a car being chauffeured to a state of nervous anxiety. A Lawrence Welk fan would undoubtedly have gone completely berserk.

I thought we'd never reach the house, and peace and quiet. But if I had known what I was in for, I might rather have endured the car.

The feast set before us was worthy of a king—or a condemned man who had been granted his last request. Conversation was pleasant and casual. The usual niceties were discussed and the proverbial questions posed.

"How did you and Kathy meet?"

"How long have you been married?"

"Do you have any children?"

"Why don't . . ."

Fortunately they managed to bite their tongues on the last question.

Kathy and I were seated with both parents on our left and the teenage driver directly opposite us. The atmosphere seemed a little tense, but I dismissed it merely as apprehension at having new guests in the home.

I was wrong. The whole meal had been arranged to resolve a long-standing parental confrontation. Finally, about halfway through the meal, the mother folded her arms. Leaning back in her chair, she posed what was supposed to be a nonchalant question. Her acting skills would never have won an Academy Award. The faked composure couldn't conceal the belligerency in her voice.

"Brother Larson," she began. (The formal address should have alerted me. I insist on being called just Bob.) "Don't you think that when parents tell their children not to listen to certain kinds of music that they should obey?"

The son slid down slowly in his chair. He knew it was coming, but the question was still embarrassing. Food suddenly became unpalatable to him. His fork made endless designs in the mashed potatoes during the silence that followed.

Mom waited expectantly. After all, didn't Bob Larson speak against the evils of rock music? Hadn't she invited him to vindicate this long-standing feud with her son? Wouldn't he reply with an emphatic "Yes!" and set the wayward child in his place once and for all?

I waited for what must have seemed an eternity to both of them. But I needed Solomon's wisdom, and it wasn't coming that quickly. Finally, I decided to be truly Christlike. When the Pharisees asked Jesus a question, he posed them one in return. "Answer mine and I'll answer yours," he would say.

Swallowing my slowly chewed bite of food, and glancing at my wife for moral support, I knew the time for a reply had come.

"Please answer a question for me first," I said to the mother. "Do you love your son?"

She was stunned and insulted. How dare I put her on the spot. Guests were supposed to be more polite than that. She wanted endorsement, not harassment. What a question to ask a mother. Her dislike for my response was covered by the same thespian inabilities that had failed to hide her belligerency.

"What do you mean?" she asked. "I brought him into the world, didn't I? I cook his meals and provide for him. He's supposed to honor and obey me."

"That's not an answer," I insisted.

Gradually, the intent of my inquiry hit home. Her body relaxed, and she hung her head slightly.

"Yes," she answered. "I do love my son."

"Well then," I probed further, "when was the last time you told him?"

Tears welled in her eyes. She had brought me there to put her son on the spot and she had gotten the hot seat.

I glanced at her son who could scarcely hide his glee at seeing Mom get hers. He forgot his mashed potatoes in the satisfaction of seeing Mom put on the defensive. But he shouldn't have gloated so readily. He was about to get his.

"Do you love your parents?" I asked him.

Now his head hung too. Having the shoe on the other foot wasn't as much fun.

I barely heard the "Yes" he muttered under his breath. But it was an audible enough answer to warrant my next question.

"When was the last time you told them?"

Through the mist that was forming in his eyes he looked across the table toward his parents. Almost simultaneously the three of them exploded in a torrent of tears. Kathy and I sat quietly, unembarrassed by this long-neglected emotional display of affection between parent and child.

When the crying and expressione of sorrow and regret had died down, I felt impressed to carry my point further.

"Do you know what the problem is in this home? No communication," I answered rhetorically.

"I've never been to your house, but I can tell you what happens every night. You eat a hurried meal and split in different directions. You head for the TV," I said, looking at Mom and Dad, "to be entertained in the way that pleases you. Then," I went on, referring to the son, "you head for your bedroom to turn on the stereo."

I again directed my attention to the parents. "About an hour later that beat from the music pounding through the ceiling gets on your nerves so you yell up the stairs, 'Turn that junk down!' "

The parents nodded in agreement.

"Then," I said to the son, "knowing how much it irritates Mom, you turn it up all the louder."

The son grinned sheepishly. Obviously I had hit the nail on the head.

"An hour later," I added, "the music gets on your nerves even more, so you yell up the stairs again."

"And you," I said to the son who was getting more fidgety, "just turn it up again all the louder."

My analysis was nearly complete.

"The problem in this home is not the kind of music your son is listening to. The problem is a lack of communication. You both live in separate environments and scream across the barriers of the generation gap. The only time you talk is to let each other know how objectionable the life style of the other is."

More was said, but I'll not bore you with the complete sermon text; however, before we left that day, we had all joined hands around the table for a time of prayer to heal the scars of a wounded home.

I hadn't known at the time, but the young man we were eating with had never become a Christian. That very Sunday evening, at the conclusion of my message, I issued an invitation for those who had never accepted the Lord. He was the first one to step forward.

This story is not an isolated illustration. Many homes are just the same. I constantly encounter parents who are alarmed at their children's musical tastes. For some of them it's merely the sound of rock that is objectionable. It's loud and noisy and so unlike the mellower sounds to which they are accustomed.

Parents may be vaguely aware of some dangers in the rock scene through general knowledge. But their concern is seldom expressed in a constructive manner. Often it tends to be high-handed or uptight. Sometimes it's downright overbearing. Such actions only compound the problems. Believe me, if your child has absorbed rebellious attitudes fostered by the morals of Led Zeppelin, belatedly imposing musical censorship will only make matters worse.

Fortunately, there is a way out of this dilemma. As a parent, you can establish Christ-honoring musical norms for your family. Teenagers can be taught to use discretion in their musical tastes and please God as well as Mom and Dad. It won't be an easy issue to confront, but the spiritual future of your home may depend upon it.

TWO
LET'S SPEND
THE NIGHT TOGETHER

In 1954 a Cleveland disc jockey by the name of Alan Freed
was searching for a term to describe the response of teenagers who
had gone wild over a new musical fad. Concerts by Chuck
Berry and Gene Vincent were accompanied by riots of violence
and sexual hysteria. Millions of female eyes were glued
to the groin of Elvis. A sexual as well as a musical revolution was
taking place.

Finally, Freed found his phrase. From the ghetto community
he borrowed a descriptive expression referring to fornication: rock
and roll. The name stuck, and the music lived on. But the
lyrics of rock and roll were to explore fringes of lyrical pornography
that even Freed never dreamed of.

Adults who are a little naive regarding the debauchery in the
content of many of today's pop hits may react with a "so what?"
attitude.

"Things were bad in our day too," they may say. "Didn't
the girls swoon over Sinatra? And what about Cole Porter's 'Let's
Do It'?"

It's true that Porter slyly suggested doing what the birds and
bees do. But he was quick to safely add an explanation:
"Let's do it—let's fall in love."

Many of today's popular songs leave no such excusable options.
The old hack about "crooning a tune in the month of June
under the moon" gave way to "Let's Spend the Night Together" in

the sixties and "I Want to Kiss You All Over" in the seventies.

Love means sex to most contemporary rock composers.
Meaningful relationships are often described as fruitless and
painful. In "Two Out of Three Ain't Bad" the singer laments his
ejection from a lover's bed. She assures him she wants
and needs him, but goes on to say that love is out of the question.
Oh well, the singer concludes, at least the act of sex itself
was worth it, because "two out of three..."

In other words, love has a single dimension—desire. Lust is
the motivation and conquest is the goal. That's why the
singer for Foreigner declares he is "hot blooded" for a one night
stand with whom he can stay "all night." Rod Stewart is
equally insistent when he admonishes, "Tonight's the Night." His
angelic virgin lover is told to spread her wings because
Stewart wants to "come inside."

The mere titles of songs over the last several years would make
a sailor blush. Try these recent top ten hits: "Let's Make
a Baby," "Do Something Freaky," "Afternoon Delight," "Sharing
the Night Together," "Hot Child in the City," "You Never
Done It Like That," "Nobody Does It Better," "Lay Down Sally,"
"I'm In You," "Torn Between Two Lovers."

Nothing is left to the imagination. Every intimate detail
pertaining to the physical aspects of sex is thoroughly explained
to the teenage mind. "Thunder Island" describes two naked
bodies lying in the sun. "Oh, What a Night" tells of a young man's
first sexual encounter, with the admission that the singer
didn't even know her name. Led Zeppelin in "Trampled Under
Foot" refers to a girl's "transmission" as having hot oil flowing
while the singer suggests that he'd like to pump some gas.

Another singer speaks of the V.D. he collected on a trip as a
"souvenir" which he can't declare at customs. "Only the Good Die
Young" by Billy Joel laments the fact that Catholic girls
stay virgins much too long.

The graphics of album jackets themselves are often decidedly
pornographic. The parent who is certain his son would never
read *Playboy* nor his daughter digest *Playgirl* is in for a shock when
he thumbs through the average teenager's stack of records.

"Wild Cherry" features the close-up view of a twelve-inch-wide
pair of lips, suggestively parted to bite a cherry. Montrose
recorded an album called "Jump on It" with a jacket that pictures

front and back views of a sparsely clothed female crotch.

The Ohio Players have deliberately exploited nudity to sell records. An album entitled "Angel" unfolds to show a full-length, buxom nude. Another album incites voyeuristic fantasies by picturing a nude covered with honey. But they may have reached their limit with a third album with shades of bestiality, showing a voluptuous nude suggestively nuzzling a horse.

Posters advertising such releases are equally obscene. What teenager could turn down a chance to purchase an album advertised by these scenes: an hermaphrodite (Al Kooper's "Act Like Nothing's Wrong"); a close up of frilly but scanty panties (a record by artist Jorge Santana); a girl with her legs spread apart suggestively licking an appropriately shaped ice cream cone (Faze-O's "Good Thang"); Henry Gross stroking the body of a nude woman lying on a bed ("Show Me the Stage"); three women in undergarments lying on top of each other ("Take the Heat Off Me," by Bony M); Linda Rondstadt in a see-through peasant dress ("Hasten Down the Wind").

If this frank and explicit portrayal of sexuality already has you in a state of shock, hang on. You don't know the code language by which the more explicit lyrical images are conveyed. Terms like "engine," "motor" and "machine" are all sexual euphemisms. Try this lexicon on for size: "funky" refers to sexual odors; "gig" is a reference to sex orgies; "groovy" is a description of the physical position of intercourse, "groupies" are prostitutes who ply their wares in the company of rock stars; "get off" signifies the goal of lovemaking.

While it is true that such terms have been adopted in wider usage of the vernacular, the teenagers who know their original meaning listen to such language with a chuckle and a sneer. They know that Mom and Dad's moral objections to rock's lyrics have been cleverly circumvented. It's no wonder that one rock periodical refers to these trends as "prophylactic rock."[1] Sex-oriented tunes are also sometimes referred to in the music industry as "masturbatory rock."

With such exploitation of suggestive themes, a parent can only worry what comes next. The answer is, "It gets worse!"

Parents should know that the examples in this book aren't the worst ones. Some top hits are so lewd that the lyrics can't be printed for fear of having this book classified as pornography.

Having explored every possible moral limit to excite and titillate, rock composers had only one place left to go: sadomasochism (the inflicting of physical pain for sexual pleasure).

Any teenager can easily verify that the groups and songs discussed are not from the lesser-known end of the musical spectrum. The songs and singers referred to represent the most popular groups with songs at the top of the charts. These are well-known entertainers who don't need perversion to sell records. They give the impression that they practice what they preach.

Bad Company sang in "Heartbeat" about tying up a lover to beat her. When the singer suggests she call the doctor, she replies that she gets her kicks that way. A Los Angeles Sunset Strip poster advertising the Rolling Stones' album "Black and Blue" displayed a scantily-clad, voluptuous woman with her legs spread apart, literally beaten black and blue. The Stones' album "Some Girls" features songs like, "When the Whip Comes Down," and "Beast of Burden." "Am I rough enough?" Mick Jagger sings in the latter.

Ted Nugent is pictured on his album "Cat Scratch Fever" with his lover's hands literally ripping him bloody. KISS dresses appropriately in chains and leather, the tools of sadomasochistic bondage. They sing of keeping a whip handy and promise to teach the pleasures of love in a "different way." The ultimate expression of a no-holds-barred approach to love was perhaps echoed by the Blue Oyster Cult. In their song "Don't Fear the Reaper," they advocate a teenage love-pact of suicide.

Who's to blame for all of this? Who is it that is providing such warped ideas for young minds to consume?

It's the dollar-conscious adults who run the major record companies. Driven by greed and avarice, they care nothing about the morals of your children. They will stoop to any depth to arouse the sexual curiosity of teenagers. But there have to be people willing to write and record such trash.

It is the artists themselves who convey without compunction the message that sex has no moral limitations. Composer/ producer/artist Johnny Bristol says, "Sex is where it's at in music . . . and I like it."[2]

Singer John Oates agrees, declaring that rock and roll is "99 percent sex."[3]

One rock periodical ran a series of interviews with rock stars
who detailed their personal sex habits. Blondie's Debby
Harry revealed she uses the rhythm method with her multiple
partners. The Tube's Fee Waybill explained that he always checks
the birth control method used by fifteen-year-olds before
seducing them.[4]

Even the names of rock groups illustrate sexual overtones.
Steely Dan is named after a male dildo and 10 C.C. has
their name calculated on the basis of being one cubic centimeter
more than the average male emission.

Perhaps your ears have already turned enough shades of blue.
You'd rather not hear such things in a family-oriented book. But
please remember, these are the groups *your* children may
be listening to, and these are facts that they may already be
familiar with.

It's not this book you need to fear, but rather the rock idols that
teens look to as oracles of wisdom reflecting on life or love.
David Krebs, manager of Aerosmith, explains, "When you're in a
certain frame of mind, particularly sexually oriented, there's
nothing better than rock and roll. Because that's where most of the
performers are at."[5]

Disco artist Donna Summer is living proof of that analysis. Her
first hit, "Love to Love You Baby," was a seventeen-minute
vinyl aphrodisiac. It consisted of her repetitious moaning of the
title phrase over and over to the accompaniment of rapturous
groans and murmurs in a marathon of twenty-two orgasms.

In fact, sex is so important in selling records that a special
preview house has been set up in L.A. where new songs
can be tested demographically. As each number is played, the
listeners can turn dials to indicate their response. Some
seats are equipped with "basal skin reponse sensors" that measure
involuntary spasms of the nervous system. The programmers
freely admit they are searching for songs that produce an orgasmic
effect and kick the needle on the meter attached to the sensors.[6]

Doug Feiger of The Knack explained the philosophy of the
group's songs this way: "We've been accused of writing about
women as sex objects, and I don't think that's so bad.
Everyone wants to be a desirable sex object. Everyone. It's a
human thing."[7] To prove their point, Feiger and friends
sing of teenage love as a "stick sweet romance" and the lustful
desires of the young man who wants to get "inside her pants."

"I've always thought that the main ingredients in rock are sex, really good stage shows, and really sassy music. Sex and sass, I really think that's where it's at," claims Debbie Harry of Blondie.[8] The lead guitarist of the group, Chris Stein, agrees. "Everybody takes it for granted rock and roll is synonymous with sex," he adds.[9]

As shocking as all of this may be to you as a parent, you're probably forced to admit that you have never heard of most of these songs and singers. You were not aware that such albums could be easily found on open display any place in your city that sells records. Worse yet, they may be in your own home. Obviously, adult ignorance is a contributing factor in allowing rock pornography to be marketed to the children in your home and community.

"Now that I know, what do I do about it?" you ask. Keep reading. Help is ahead.

FOOTNOTES

[1]*Rolling Stone*, Feb. 9, 1978, p. 100.

[2]*Billboard*, Dec. 11, 1976, p. 39.

[3]*Circus*, Jan. 31, 1976, p. 39.

[4]*Ibid.*, Feb. 20, 1976, p. 24.

[5]*Ibid.*, October 17, 1978, p. 34.

[6]*Time*, Dec. 29, 1975, p. 39.

[7]*Rolling Stone*, Oct. 18, 1979, p. 37.

[8]*Hit Parader*, Sept. 1979, p. 31.

[9]*People*, May 21, 1979.

THREE
A CHIP OFF THE OLD BLOCK

"Your son acts just like you," Mom says.

Whether that comment has come from frustration or admiration, the result is the same. Dad secretly feels a flush of pride. He wants his son to be like him. But for some parents, that flush has become a blush. The Gay Revolution is upon us, and many a father who hoped his son would be a football hero, now discovers he would rather frequent a gay disco.

Unless you've been living in a cave in Outer Mongolia, you know only too well that today's child is threatened with homosexual influences you never had to contend with. Keeping your child straight is no longer just an assumed outcome of child-rearing, but a goal to be carefully guarded.

I have yet to meet a parent—even among the most liberal-minded—who *wanted* his child to become a homosexual. Like it or not, children are seen as a reflection of parental values. Everything is at stake in the way your child turns out. He will bring your fading years either fulfillment or heartache. He is a chip off your block. And you don't want his outcome splintered by perversion.

As a parent, you're probably disturbed when you see civic and church leaders cast a favorable attitude upon homosexuality. These men and women are in the public eye. As role models, they can't help but influence the younger generation who looks

up to them. But today's major trend-setters in the realms of style
and morality are entertainment stars.

Performers in the rock scene have the greatest influence of all
upon the values adopted by today's teenager. With homosexuals
coming out of the closet for a frontal assault on society's
morals, it was inevitable that rock, as a cultural reflection, would
deal with gay pride.

The rock interest in homosexuality is not entirely recent in
origin. Several years ago the Kinks took a fling at homosexuality
and sexual ambiguity with a song called "Lola" describing
a homosexual who walked like a woman and talked like a man. The
leader of the group, Ray Davies, who wrote the song,
often deliberately gives a homosexually oriented performance.
In like manner Frank Zappa and the Mothers of Invention
were exploring bisexual themes as early as the mid-sixties. For the
cover of one album, they were pictured in women's clothing.

One L.A. nightclub features gay country singers. A reporter
described a male cowboy in black nylons, lipstick, mascara,
rouge, and boots singing, "What Made Milwaukee Famous
Made a Loser Out of Me."

Various artists have recently gotten into the homosexual bag.
Before his death, Keith Moon of The Who frequently
appeared in public wearing women's clothing. When the gay-rock
trend was first beginning, the Dolls, a New York City rock
band, sported members such as Johnny Thunder on guitar, who
wore red leather cowboy chaps with fringes. Lead singer
David Johansen wore skin-tight trousers and platform heels, while
bass guitarist Arthur Kane appeared in pink tights. Even
Mick Jagger of the Rolling Stones now comes out on stage with
mascara to further flaunt his often suggested and well-known
bisexual ambiguities.

The Tubes, a Bay area group, combine music with perversion
and theatrics. The band consists of several semi-nude dancers and
a lead singer who calls himself Quay Lewd (named after
the sedative drug Quaalude). A and M Records plowed $350,000
into their act which sold out auditoriums night after night.
While singing tunes like "Don't Touch Me There," they distribute
phony cocaine to the audience with a literal snow shovel.
Each song is interspersed with public fondling and masochistic
overtones.

Among the best known gay rock entertainers are Lou

21 A Chip off the Old Block

Reed and David Bowie. Reed, a former member of the
Velvet Underground (a rock act produced by the self-proclaimed
homosexual Andy Warhol) sings about bleak visions of a
nightmare world dominated by drugs. He has become one of the
foremost gay rock entertainers with albums like "Transformer."
Reed is pictured on the jacket in high heels, panty hose,
rouge, and mascara. Some of the songs included on the album are,
"Make-up" (a tune about dolling up and coming out of the
closets "into the streets") and "Good-night Ladies," which tells of
the lonely Saturday nights that a perfumed homosexual
spends. In another song entitled "Vicious," he describes hitting
his lover with a stick during sexual relationships.

David Bowie, who records for RCA Victor, is a British singer/
composer/guitarist who boasts in interviews and songs that
he is bisexual. His wife is an admitted lesbian, and out of their
union have come two children. Wearing orange-hued hair
and laced high-heeled boots, he moves in female fashion to a rock
beat. Bowie often pretends acts of copulation on stage with
other males while singing songs about homosexuals such as
"Queen Bitch." In spite of such perverted extravagance, he has
been a major superstar in this era, and his concerts are
sellouts wherever he goes. But the wealth and fame his perversion
has brought seems to have only resulted in depression.
One rock magazine reported that Bowie had expressed the desire
to have a tragic death before he hit thirty—that this would
have been the perfect ending to his career.

A gay label, Olivia Records, has been formed to market lesbian
albums with songs like "Gay and Proud" and "Women
Loving Women." Before their professional demise, the female trio
Labelle appealed to a highly adorned gay following. As
singer Nona Hendryx put it, "I like appealing to both men and
women. I don't limit myself. I'm all sexes."[1]

Cindy Bullens, a rising female star, says, "I definitely feel I am
bisexual. I have never been one sex in my whole life."[2]

Even straight artists like Daryl Hall and John Oates felt obliged
to attract a gay crowd. For one album they posed for the
cover shot in heavy makeup. Hall replies, "The idea of sex with a
man doesn't turn me off. I had lots of strange experiences
with older boys between when I was four to fourteen."[3]

Todd Rundgren joined the bandwagon by adding multicolored
hues to his shoulder-length locks. A sadomasochistic group, the

Cycle Sluts, struts onstage in corsets and black lingerie.

Some gay groups and singers have been able to achieve only limited success. Jobriath was heralded as the ultimate gay star. He declared, "I'm a true fairy. I'm selling sex."[4] But the public didn't buy his paeans to homosexual love.

Steve Grossman was heralded as the "Bob Dylan of the gay movement." Mercury records made him the first gay minstrel promoted by a major label with the release of "Caravan Tonight." Singer Tom Robinson combines homosexuality and politics. The logo of his band features a clenched fist and the record sleeves of his albums contain information about a gay switchboard that advises young homosexuals on how to come out of the closet. Robinson's odes to perversion include "Let My People Be" and "Glad to Be Gay."

David Bowie was responsible (it was to be expected) for helping to launch the careers of artists like Eno, Iggy Pop (who was arrested for female impersonation), and Wayne County.

County, the most outrageous, appears in full drag with a purple wig and rhinestone studded bathrobe. He declares, "I always wanted to be a homecoming queen. I was such an unlucky little girl." He typifies the depravity of the gay rock scene by comments like, "Jesus Christ was a strange boy Himself."[5] County's songs include tunes such as "It Takes a Man Like Me to Like a Woman Like Me."

County was outdone only by the absurdity of British star Alex Harvey who proclaimed, "Homosexuality is a good thing. It stops the population from getting any bigger."[6]

Mick Ronson was, for a while, David Bowie's lead guitarist. Bowie would sometimes get on his knees to play Ronson's guitar with his tongue (with obvious phallic overtones). When asked how he minded such antics, Ronson replied, "I took my bisexual image seriously. I didn't like it at first, but then you get used to it. With so many people around you being bisexual, you get used to it for yourself."[7]

All the gay rock groups have to go a long way to beat Alice Cooper. Alice, who claims to be the reincarnation of a seventeenth-century witch,[8] began his rock career by coming out on stage dressed with mascara and in women's clothing. An Alice Cooper performance is a wedding of perversion and dramatized violence as Alice chops a lifelike doll to pieces, makes love to a writhing snake, and eventually hangs himself on a gallows. In spite of all this, Alice was asked to lecture at the Eastman School of Music in Rochester, New York. His subject was the art of writing popular music.

Once a man charged the stage and tried to kill Alice during a concert. He managed to hit Cooper over the head with a beer bottle. On another occasion an M-80 bomb exploded after being thrown onstage. Once his drummer found blood flowing down his back, only to discover he had been stabbed by darts hurled from the audience.

The Cooper album, "Billion Dollar Babies," had already earned over a million dollars on advance sales before it hit the stands. Included is the song, "I Love the Dead," an anthem of necrophilia which Alice sings while simulating sex onstage with a lifelike mannequin. Cooper's album "Muscle of Love" was planned to include a painting of the group seated at a Thanksgiving dinner in a whorehouse.

Rock artists such as Cooper appear to live rich, successful, and happy lives. That itself is a powerful moral statement favoring homosexuality. No matter how much you've trained your child to disdain sexual perversion, the constant onslaught of the media can take its toll. Your child may "know" it's wrong to be a homosexual, but will that predisposition endure when he's told day after day by his rock idols that gay is good?

Parents need to be rudely awakened. The storm troopers for gay liberation are attacking with guitars in hand. Certainly not all rock artists are gay. But those who do practice homosexuality represent a disproportionate share when compared with society-at-large. This imbalanced and favorable inclination can have a subliminally disastrous effect on the young person who digs the music of such artists.

It's sad that in some homes the son isn't a chip off his Dad's block. Rather, he's been re-whittled to more closely resemble the progeny of David Bowie. If you don't want that to happen in your home, this book is designed to help you.

FOOTNOTES

[1]*Rolling Stone*, July 3, 1975, p. 43.

[2]*Ibid.*, April 5, 1979, p. 23.

[3]*Ibid.*, April 21, 1977, p. 15.

[4]*Ibid.*

[5]*Hit Parader*, June 19, 1975, p. 71.

[6]*Circus*, July, 1975.

[7]*Ibid.*, August, 1975, p. 70.

[8]*Ibid.*, December 19, 1978, p. 23.

FOUR
WHERE DID WE GO WRONG?

Knock. Knock.

"Honey, wake up." You try to rouse your husband. "There's someone at the door."

You fumble for the light switch. It's midnight. Who would be calling on you at this hour? It couldn't be your daughter. She said she'd be staying overnight with a friend.

Finally, both of you are awake and headed for the front door. You open it and there stands your daughter, next to a police officer. What could she have done wrong? She can't even look at you. Her head is hung in shame.

For a moment, there's a stunned silence. Then it's broken by the officer saying, "I've just picked up your daughter driving under the influence of drugs. We'll have to take her in and book her. Would you like to come along?"

In ten seconds your whole world has fallen apart. Other parents have problems with children who take drugs. But not you. Yours is a Christian home. Why, you've raised her in church and Sunday school. This must be a dream. It can't be true.

Suddenly, you realize the police officer is waiting for an answer.

"Yes, we'll come with you. Won't you come in and have a seat while we get ready?"

The two of you hardly look at each other while you dress. But the occasional glances reveal the same question on both of your faces: "Where did we go wrong?"

All the plans and hopes for your daughter have been crushed. The rest of her life she'll bear a stigma, and maybe a jail record. Now, her future is a big question mark. The family reputation has been tarnished. People will look at you with one thought in mind. You've failed as a parent.

As all these fears come crashing in on you, there's still one question you've got to have answered: "Where *did* we go wrong?"

Before you sink any further into self-condemnation, you've got to realize that probing your past role as a parent will do no good. The chances are you have tried to raise your child properly. However, there's one reason for your daughter's disaster that you may never find no matter how much guilt you inveigh against yourself.

You may be under the false assumption that your training, example, and advice were the major influence in your child's life. But I've got news for you. Someone else has had her ears and mind more than you have. There's someone she learns more from in one day than she hears from you in a week. And that someone isn't a teacher, her pastor, or a schoolmate.

Stop and think for a moment. What is she tuned in to more than anything else? That's right. Her music!

You may have done your best as a parent, but it's hard to counter that constant absorption of pro-drug attitudes coming across through today's music. It's all there in the words of the songs and the public image of the rock stars whose records your child listens to. It may be hard to accept, but face it. How that entertainer feels about doing dope may mean more to some teenagers than the advice of their own parents.

Just what kind of drug philosophy is found in the rock generation? The rise of the hippie movement in the late sixties encouraged a rash of songs with a persuasive attitude toward drugs. Some songs openly advocated turning on while others simply talked about drugs without making any moral comments. Fortunately, most of those earlier songs have faded from the scene, but the latter still remain.

It might be argued that merely mentioning drugs in a song doesn't necessarily convey approval. However, such casual discussion of drug usage tends to raise the subject of dope to a level of common acceptance and familiarity. It's like advertising. The desirability of a product to the consumer market is directly proportionate to the frequency of its mention.

When the Rolling Stones sing about "Sister Morphine," and "Sweet Cousin Cocaine," it's pretty hard for the average thirteen-year-old to see beyond the endorsement in the self-dramatizing tone of the lyrics.

In the sixties, drug-rock songs declared that youth should take a "Magic Carpet Ride" or a "Journey to the Center of Your Mind." The Beatles sang, "I get high with a little help from my friends." The fact that the latter song has become a pop standard says something about how our whole culture has become desensitized to off-the-cuff drug references.

At a recent International Music Conference, the spokesman for a major record industry advertising firm stated: "Record companies and music publishers have earned many millions of dollars from extolling the virtues of drugs. Would one turn out phonograph records extolling the virtues of forceful rape, armed robbery, or kidnapping? The answer, I think, for many companies is 'yes' as long as there is money in it, and they don't go to jail."

A prominent rock manager stated, "No matter what anyone tells you, drugs will always be part of the rock scene."[1]

Robert Forbes, a rock critic, summed up his appraisal of rock and drugs in this way: "Drugs are a necessary ingredient for many rock musicians. It is almost impossible to sustain the frantic pace, ungodly hours and inhuman energy without resorting to some kind of drug. The rock musician thrives on the periphery of that high and uses it as a crutch to hold his position, audience and individuality."[2]

The biggest influence promoting drugs in the current rock scene is the image of the singers, not the songs. Cocaine is openly snorted at recording studios and is as accepted as alcohol when it's time to celebrate the signing of a contract. The attitude of many entertainers gives the impression that turning on is no big deal. Being arrested for drug violations is almost fashionable in some rock circles, and certainly nothing unusual. Consequently, if your child has been attending the concerts of such artists, and he is later offered a dose of dope, he may well remember it as something Mick Jagger or Gregg Allman has used and enjoyed.

Tragically, the possible drug conviction of your child won't be shrugged off as easily as that of John Lennon or Keith Richards. A major disc jockey put it this way: "Most of the artists I talked to refused to be anti-cocaine because they use it."[3]

You may be warning your child against the dangers of drugs, but listen to what his rock heroes are telling him:

"I can sing better after shooting smack [heroin] in both arms than after eating too much."—Linda Rondstadt.[4]

"We were sitting, passing around a joint—a doobie—so we called ourselves the Doobie Brothers."—Tom Johnston of the Doobie Brothers.[5]

"I'm in the music business for the sex and narcotics."—Glenn Fry of the Eagles.[6]

"We avoid all hard drugs like cocaine although we do smoke marijuana now and again."—the Bee Gees.[7]

Every year, thousands of young people die from drug overdoses. Some of them—maybe your child—might never have turned on were it not for the condoning attitudes of some major rock artists. Are these irresponsible entertainers acting as accomplices in drug-related deaths? Are their record albums an artistic achievement or a sermon resulting in addiction to mind-bending chemicals?

A listing of prominent rock artists who have openly admitted drug usage would be too lengthy to recount. Some more notable examples would include Jerry Garcia, Jimmy Buffett, Stephen Stills, Leon Russell, Joe Cocker, Eric Clapton, and Johnny Winter. Both Keith Richards of the Rolling Stones and Gregg Allman have been charged with heroin possession. Mick Jagger of the Stones was feted with a birthday party in Madison Square Garden. His present was a silver-plated snuff box for cocaine.

The saddest commentary on the rock-drug scene is written in the last chapter of the lives of those drug zealots who were finally done in by what they glorified. Rock stars are caught up in a false world of fast cars and large sums of money. Theirs is an unreal existence of over-indulgence brought on by wealth and stardom. Many have burned out in their prime.

Jimi Hendrix ushered in the drug-death syndrome when he suffocated in a pool of his own vomit from an overdose. Within weeks, Janis Joplin and Jim Morrison followed him to a similar fate. Brian Jones of the Stones drowned in his private pool while presumably high.

Five musicians even had plastic surgery to reshape their faces to look like Hendrix, Joplin, and Morrison. They billed their act as "Rock and Roll Heaven" and set up a tour of forty-one cities.

Drug overdoses were also credited as the cause of death for Al Wilson of Canned Heat, Gram Parsons and Gary Thain of Uriah Heep, Vinnie Taylor of Sha Na Na, and Keith Moon of The Who, and Lowell George of Little Feat.

It was not just casual drug usage that brought about such tragedies. In most instances death was due to multiple overdoses of pot, cocaine, barbiturates, and alcohol. Heroin, the dreaded drug most rock stars claim to eschew, was the killer of Tommy Bolin of Deep Purple, Robbie McIntosh of the Average White Band, and Sid Vicious of the Sex Pistols.

These names probably mean little to most of you parents. But let your teenager read this chapter and he'll tell you that these people were top performers in the rock world. Their names, which are anonymous to parents, are known to every youth in the land. These are the idols who told your child to turn on in the first place.

For every rock star done in by dope, another comes along to claim the cause. But what of the dead? Who purchased their records and supported their drug habits? Who yelled for another encore and pushed the pressures of stardom beyond the limits of endurance? Their fans, that's who. Maybe your own son or daughter.

What really killed these talented but undisciplined musicians? The drug or the demands of the public who drove them to it? It's a point worth making to your child before he buys another album of an artist devoted to dope.

Encouraging your child to boycott the music of artists who advocate or use drugs is a moral action that would save this generation a lot of misery. It also might save your family from that midnight knock on the door.

FOOTNOTES

[1]*Circus*, April 17, 1979, p. 16.

[2]*Ibid.*, April 17, 1979, p. 16.

[3]*Rolling Stone*, November 22, 1973.

[4]*Ibid.*, March 27, 1975.

[5]*Ibid.*, January 4, 1973, p. 16.

[6]*People*, June 30, 1975, p. 60.

[7]*Circus*, August 3, 1973, p. 38.

FIVE
DEPROGRAMMING YOUR CHILD

"Good afternoon, sir," she says, smiling broadly. "My name is Laurie."

The pedestrian is taken aback for a moment. *Nobody* smiles or stops to speak on a busy city street. What's she up to? But before that question can be answered, she pins a bright red carnation on his lapel.

"I represent an organization that feeds starving children in the Third World," she informs the bewildered man. "Could you make a donation to our worthy cause?"

That fresh smile and pleading look has gotten to him. After all, who wouldn't trust such an innocent-looking young lady?

He reaches into his pocket and pulls out a dollar bill.

"Don't you have something larger? Babies are dying every day because we don't have enough food to give them."

For a moment he ponders the request. She's right. A dollar sure won't buy much these days. And this young solicitor does look so trustworthy.

Screeeech!!

A sedan pulls up to the curb. The doors fly open and two men jump out. One of them clamps his hand over Laurie's mouth while the other twists her arms into a hammerlock.

The pedestrian, in the process of reaching for a larger donation, is stunned. He watches as Laurie is forcibly shoved into the car. The doors slam and the woman driver speeds away, careening through the traffic.

What should he do? It all looks like something out of a TV detective show. Should he run for help to the nearest policeman?

He could, but it really wouldn't do any good. Those two men were her father and brother, and the driver was her mother. This was not a kidnap but an abduction. The car is now on its way to a motel where a professional deprogrammer waits.

That smiling young lady? She's a member of a religious cult and has forsaken all to follow her guru. The temple she attends is now the legal owner of her worldly possessions and the controlling force in her life.

Her own parents haven't seen her since the day she disappeared a year ago. No letters, no phone calls, nothing. If it hadn't been for a friend who recognized her in this distant city, Laurie might never have been found.

This past year has been agony for her parents. The loss of their child was bad enough. But the guilt was even worse. How could this have happened to their daughter?

They had read every book they could find about cults. The brainwashing techniques interested them most: "love-bombing," low-protein diets, sensory deprivation, little sleep, and the constant indoctrination of cult leaders.

Still, it was hard to believe that even these tactics could have so quickly transformed Laurie's beliefs and character. One question had nagged at them those long twelve months. Was there something in her past which had affected her thinking and made her susceptible to the teachings of this cult?

These distraught parents searched everywhere for a clue. Friends and school teachers were quizzed. Laurie's pastor was consulted. The books she read and every movie she'd gone to see was suspect. But try as they might, they could not uncover anything she had absorbed that could so alter her.

However, in their searching, these concerned parents overlooked one place: Laurie's bedroom. In one corner sat a record player. Underneath it was a huge collection of rock albums.

Her parents never cared much for the kind of music Laurie listened to. They dismissed her interest as a passing teenage fad. The philosophy and life styles of her rock heroes were never the subject of scrutiny. Too bad. One look at her favorite records would have uncovered a major culprit in Laurie's conversion to the world of the cults.

Those vinyl pressings and cardboard jackets were more than a

mere form of entertainment. Through them, the religious
philosophies of the East were meeting the teenage mind of the
West. And in the process, Kipling's dictum, "Ne'er the
twain shall meet," was being reduced to shambles.

Just what records were in Laurie's library?

An album by the Moody Blues was at the front. Its title, "In
Search of the Lost Chord," refers to the mystical concept
of a musical chord with vibrations that have supernatural
properties. If that exact chord can be struck, the hearer may obtain
instantaneous enlightenment through the transcendent state
of mind it creates.

The inside of the album jacket pictures a *yantra*, the visual
equivalent of the *mantra* in Transcendental Meditation. An
explanation is provided as to the Hindu and yogic background of
the *yantra*. While the record is being played, the listener
is told to stare at the geometric designs, and thereby enter an
altered state of consciousness. In fact, God is declared to
be embodied in the very sound of the Hindu Sanskrit word "OM,"
the title of one cut from the album.

The rest of Laurie's records reveal a similar vein of eastern
religious viewpoints. An album by the popular group Yes is
entitled "Tales from Topographic Oceans." The jacket explains
that the lyrics are based on the Hindu Scriptures and were
specifically inspired by the reading of Paramahansa Yogananda's
book *Autobiography of a Yogi*. The songs of the album are
said to reveal "the science of God," the tantric sexual rituals, and
reincarnation.

Whatever confusion may be left by the oblique lyrics of rock
songs is often dispelled by the clear instructions on the
album jacket. One such example is The Strawbs record "Grave
New World." Included is a quotation from the Buddha as
well as a prayer of praise dedicated to the Egyptian sun god Ra.

A wide variety of other rock artists have entertained a
serious or flirting interest in eastern religions. England Dan and
John Ford Coley have joined Seals and Croft in promoting
the Bahai faith. They use their concerts to overtly evangelize, and
Coley who has been a member for six years adds, "I had a
strong Christian background."[1]

Another group is named after the Hindu god of destruction,
Shiva. They are called Shiva's Headband.

One of the most zealous rock artists to espouse transcendental

thought is the British star Gary Wright. Another follower
of Paramahansa Yogananda (mentioned earlier), he spoke in his hit
"Dream Weaver" of traveling to astral planes (out-of-the-body
experiences). His tunes are composed while meditating
daily under a pyramid. He acknowledges that before his concerts
he performs *kriya* yoga (a highly spiritistic branch of yoga).

Mike Love of the Beach Boys has practiced TM for more
than a decade. He claims to have fasted to the extent he attempted
communication with nature and birds. Donovan, an early
devotee of the Maharishi Mahesh Yogi, still defends the guru even
though the Beatles eventually rejected the Hindu mystic
whom they accused of woman-chasing. With an obvious commitment to Hindu theology, Donovan says, "What the Maharishi
laid on us is pretty strong. Truth lies in everybody. If you
meditate for years, it trains your mind to become one with the
source of thought."[2]

Shawn Phillips, the folk-rock minstrel, advocates self-control
through yoga breathing techniques. Felix Cavaliere, the
main force behind the Rascals (an early seventies rock group) also
pursues yoga and meditation as taught by Swami Satchidananda.
Cavaliere proclaims his spiritual goal is the attainment of
union with the universe.

Even John Lennon, whose espousal of radical politics has
surpassed his love for the East, managed at least one oriental hit,
"Instant Karma," based on the Hindu doctrine of cyclical
retribution.

One of the most adamant and well-publicized Hindu advocates
is John McLaughlin, guitar virtuoso of the Mahavishnu
Orchestra (a now disbanded group). The very name Mahavishnu
(McLaughlin's "spiritual" name) suggests adoration of
Vishnu, one of the trinity of major Hindu deities. McLaughlin,
who was once into heavy drugs, now lives a life of submission
to his guru, the Hindu spiritual master Sri Chinmoy.
Eight years ago, Chinmoy first came to the West, and today he
professes to serve a following of about one thousand "seekers
of Self-Realization."

As he performs, McLaughlin introduces each song with an
explanation regarding the metaphysical implications of the lyrics.
The audience is asked to join in a moment of meditation.
His adoration of Chinmoy surpasses most typical guru worship. "I

am immersed in him," he explains. "He is a Divine Being. Perfection. Through the grace of Sri Chinmoy, I've become more aware of the real presence of the Supreme Being."[3] Such worship is monetary as well, and much of Mahavishnu's income is devoted to Chinmoy. As McLaughlin explains, "My guru know how to spend my money better than I do."

Can such devotion lead to involvement with evil forces? McLaughlin admits as much when he describes the inspiration for his music. He declares, "When I let the spirit play me, it's an intense delight. My role as a musician is to make everyone aware of his own divinity."[4]

On another occasion, McLaughlin was even more specific regarding the inspiration of his performances. "One night we were playing," he says, "and suddenly the spirit entered into me, and I was playing, but it was no longer me playing."[5]

The band, Mahavishnu, gave way to another group called Shakti (the Hindu goddess who supposedly resides at the base of the spine and is released through the posturing positions of yoga).

McLaughlin is responsible for turning on Carlos Santana (leader of the popular latin-rock group Santana) to Chinmoy. Carlos, who used to dig wine and grass, now opts for meditating with candles and a picture of his new guru. He claims to have increased devotion for Christ (whom McLaughlin believes lives in everybody), but has, in contrast, adopted a Hindu name. He prefers now to be called Devadip, meaning, "The lamp of the light of the Supreme." Santana says of his new faith, "It was like being born again."[6] He has since gone on tour and recorded an album with John McLaughlin, all to spread the guru's light.

After looking through these albums, Laurie's parents would have begun to understand how she could so readily convert to a strange religious cult. The fact is, the cult's teachings weren't really all that strange. Every element of their doctrine and belief structure were concepts Laurie already had an easy familiarity with. What she now was being taught daily at the temple, she had previously absorbed daily in her own bedroom.

But Laurie's favorite artist was George Harrison. It was through his songs that she was most deeply steeped in the eastern view of life. Harrison's records are not only a tool of eastern evangelism, but a significant portion of the proceeds from his sales goes to support the Krishna Consciousness cult. Any traveler at an airport who has been accosted by a cult member has, undoubtedly, been solicited for a donation in exchange for a copy of *Bhagavad-Gita As It Is*, with a foreword by George Harrison.

Why is George Harrison so zealously expounding eastern mysticism? In his days with the Beatles, he turned John, Paul, and Ringo eastward to the Maharishi Mahesh Yogi. As early as 1967 Harrison was a practicing Hindu, long before the popularity of today's assorted gurus and Krishna Consciousness chanters. Since the early days of the Maharishi, his faith in Hinduism has grown. One witness to this is his composition "My Sweet Lord." The song is a prayer of dedication to Lord Krishna, an incarnation of the Hindu godhead and supposedly the god-narrator of the *Bhagavad-Gita*, the Hindu "bible." An earlier album, "All Things Must Pass," was Harrison's first solo musical excursion, and a record replete with praise of Hinduism.

To parents who may wonder as to Harrison's degree of commitment, listen to these words of evangelistic zeal published in a prominent rock periodical: "I realize now that it was the spiritual side of Indian music which attracted me in the first place. Now it is the only reason for living. The only reason for being here is to have full understanding of the spiritual aspects of life. Eastern religion taught me that the ideal is to become one with God through meditation and yoga."

On one occasion Harrison journeyed to Kali Temple in Calcutta, India. He prostrated himself before the hideous idol of the Hindu goddess of destruction, Kali, and had a replica shipped to his London mansion where it could be worshiped daily. (Kali is depicted as standing on corpses, holding a bloody severed head, and wearing a necklace of human skulls.)

One of Laurie's albums by George Harrison was entitled "Living in the Material World." The cover pictures a hand holding a symbol taken from the *Bhagavad-Gita*. Inside the album Harrison is shown wearing a clerical collar and sporting a Hindu chant button. An inner sleeve contains another large color picture of Lord Krishna, also taken from the *Gita*. Most disturbing is the message contained in the songs. Here are some examples:

"Give Me Love"—contains the line "keep me free from birth," a reference to the Hindu attempt to circumvent the reincarnation life cycles. Mr. Harrison also sings the Om chant, an utterance that is supposed to be the symbolic expression of the Hindu godhead. In reality, it is an invitation for demon manifestation.

"The Light That Has Lighted the World"—would undoubtedly be interpreted by some as being an anthem to Christ, if they are not aware of Harrison's faith in Krishna.

"Living in the Material World"—professes to have recollections of the "Spiritual Sky." The reference to such memories supports reincarnation; that supposes the ability to sometimes recall former lives. The prayer in this song is not directed toward a definitive deity but rather to the Hindu concept of an ambiguous, impersonal god that is present in all beings (Pantheism). Harrison concludes with the plea that he hopes to get out of this world by "the LORD SRI KRISHNA'S GRACE, my salvation . . ."

The remainder of the songs contain references to karma, Harrison having rejected drugs in favor of Hinduism and reincarnation.

Things seem to have gotten progressively worse for Harrison. The popularity of his music has faded in direct proportion to his mystical involvements. Harrison boldly declares, "I couldn't relate to Christ being the only son of God." In an interview he concluded, "I'm a very poor example of a spiritual person."[7] His unfulfilled search has led him into herbs, acupuncture, and Satya Sai Baba, who literally claims to be Christ. His last few albums have been duds, and he has finally been sued and found guilty for plagiarizing the melody to "My Sweet Lord."

As Harrison glibly expounds Hinduism, one can only wonder if he would also have us pray before phallic replicas of human genitals and worship sacred cows, even revering their dung as some Hindus do. Such an accusation might seem a little too harsh to some, but not to Laurie's parents.

There are many of Laurie's albums we could analyze to show the mystical implications in the songs, but all that can do little good now for her parents. It's too late. Sure, they might be able to deprogram her. However, the emotional scars left by this psychologically brutal procedure will only add to the trauma of her past in the cult. If only her parents had paid attention to the albums in her room, her story might have been different.

But maybe it's not too late for your family. A simple check of the records your child listens to may prevent heartache and disaster later.

Let's not kid ourselves that rock music is the only conveyor of eastern religious thought in our culture. Pantheism invades the philosophy of nearly every person's thinking, from environmentalists to college professors. Mysticism is heralded on television and in the press, which seems fascinated by the paranormal. Rock isn't the only offender, but it is a major one. And perhaps most dangerously, it's the one least suspected by parents.

It won't happen to your child? Are you sure? That's what the parents of scores of shaven-headed ascetics and multiplied Moonies thought too. And that's what Laurie's parents thought. Before you make the same mistake, it might be wise to check out your child's record library now.

FOOTNOTES

[1]*Rolling Stone*, April 7, 1977, p. 23.

[2]*Ibid.*, November 25, 1971.

[3]*Ibid.*, March 20, 1972, p. 26.

[4]*Newsweek*, March 27, 1972, p. 77.

[5]*Circus*, April, 1972, p. 38.

[6]*Rolling Stone*, December 30, 1976, p. 12.

[7]*Ibid.*, April 19, 1979, p. 74.

SIX
HOTEL CALIFORNIA

"As for me and my house, we will serve the Lord," Joshua said. To your Christian family, those words are probably a motto in principle, if not in fact.

You take seriously your responsibility to raise your children in the fear of the Lord. God holds you accountable for the spiritual standards of your household Knowing that, you guard carefully any intrusion of Satan into your home.

While other families watch television indiscriminately, you closely monitor the viewing habits of your children. Every day begins with devotions and ends with prayer. If your son walked in the house with *The Satanic Bible* under his arm, it would go straight to the trash can. If your daughter tried to experiment with a Ouija board in the darkness of her room, you'd stop it immediately.

But are such defensive measures sufficient for a family living in the midst of today's occult explosion? Is it possible that while you proclaim your house is the Lord's, other gods are being extolled under your very roof? Is the stereo in your child's room an altar to darkness that dispenses the devil's liturgy?

Such suppositions have the ring of fanaticism Oh, you remember the fifties when the "jungle beat" of rock and roll was reviled by clergy and musicians alike. You haven't forgotten how the twitching pelvis of Elvis was called "vulgar" and the rhythm and blues of the blacks was called "heathen."

But today, rock is heard everywhere. You are accompanied by its relentless rhythm wherever you go, in shops and restaurants, on the job, and in the car. How could anything so pervasive be so sinister? Aren't popular singers just declaring the virtues of love, albeit sometimes a little vulgar and profane?

If that's what you think, come with me on a little journey through the world of occult themes in the rock scene. Be prepared for a jolt. The vices worshiped by your generation were sex and alcohol. But some of today's entertainment heroes have added another—the devil. Before we begin our trip, let's check in for the night at a stop called "Hotel California."

The Eagles are a Southern California rock group with a country-rock blend. The band was formed on the occultic teachings of author Carlos Castaneda and nurtured with the help of peyote. They chose their name from a major spirit in the Indian cosmos.[1]

The darker side of the supernatural seems to have invaded their lyrics. In "Witchy Woman" they sing of a "restless spirit" who flies through the air with sparks flying from her fingertips. "One of These Nights" has the singer searching for "the daughter of the devil" who possesses both desires and demons.

Less explicit but possibly just as diabolical is their million-seller "Hotel California." A man driving in the desert stops for the night. He doesn't seem to be sure where he is ("This could be heaven or . . . hell"). While hearing voices in the night, he orders wine, only to be informed "that spirit" hasn't been around "since 1969." In the end he learns in terror that he can check out but he "can never leave."

"Undercover Angel," a recent hit by another singer, illustrates well the subtlety by which occult themes are introduced in the rock scene. The singer spoke of a "midnight fantasy" to whom he made love in bed. The average person probably thought the song reflected the longings of a young man who each night would dream of an imaginary lover. In fact, the song was based on the occult phenomenon of succubus, the cohabitation of a human male with a materialized demon spirit that assumes female proportions.

Shocking? But it's nothing compared to the direct involvement in the occult evidenced in the lives of some of the best-known rock and pop performers. Let's look at some examples as we continue our journey.

Before his death, Jimi Hendrix was deeply involved in the

demonic supernatural. He wore a medicine shirt from a
Hopi reservation and said he had come from an asteroid belt off
the coast of Mars. Jimi even claimed to see UFOs filling
the skies above the Woodstock rock fest.[2]

Jefferson Starship recorded a Paul Kanter song, "Your Mind
Has Left Your Body." A later album contained the song,
"Light the Sky on Fire," dedicated to "the great god Kokoa Kan."

Singer Phoebe Snow tells a chilling story of periodic
communication with a Ouija board, accompanied by her husband,
who claims to have had psychic experiences since his teens.
The board foretold her pregnancy five months in advance, and she
experienced a variety of poltergeist phenomena (e.g., shaking
beds and mirrors, the disappearance of objects). Although
this brush with demons scared her so badly she eventually
abandoned the board, she still gives psychic readings and included
a song about parapsychology ("My Faith Is Blind") on one of
her albums.[3]

Another female artist, Joni Mitchell, credits her creative
impulses to a "male muse" named Art. She feels she is married to
him and often roams naked with him on a forty-acre retreat
she owns. Her responsibility to this spirit is so strong she declares
that when he calls she will forsake lovers and even excuse
herself from parties.[4]

One of the foremost rock occultists is Ritchie Blackmore,
formerly with Deep Purple, who then split to form his own group,
Rainbow. Blackmore admits he regularly holds seances "to
get closer to God," and while he performs, he astral-projects out
of his body to float about the concert hall.[5] He records in a
seventeenth-century castle supposedly haunted by a demon who
is a servant of the 4,000-year-old Babylonian god Baal.[6]
His admitted interest in black magic has inspired songs such as
"Yoga for Health," "Stargazer" (about the slave of an Egyptian
witch), and "Tarot Woman" (about the predictions of the
occultic Tarot cards). Blackmore, famed for his temper, violence,
and moodiness, dresses appropriately in black.

Running a close second to Blackmore is Jimmy Page, lead
guitarist for Led Zeppelin. Page runs his own occult bookstore
called Equinox and is a follower of the late, infamous British
spiritualist, Aleister Crowley, a man so evil (noted for murders and
sexual perversion), he literally renamed himself "The Beast
666."[7] Crowley's mansion is now Page's home. He claims to hear

chains dragging and footsteps on the stairs. Page was asked to
compose the music for a film to be called "Lucifer Rising."
Mick Jagger had been interested in playing the role of
Lucifer. Keith Richards of the Stones was to play Beelzebub.
Convicted murderer and member of the Charles Manson
cult Bobby Beausoleil had been picked for the lead role until
it scared him so bad he quit and replaced Page as the film's
musical score composer.[8]

Fleetwood Mac, one of the most musically proficient groups on
the current scene, has likewise flirted with the occult.
Their hit "Rhiannon" was dedicated to a Welsh witch.[9] In fact, a
glance at one of their album lyric sheets reveals that most
of their songs are published by the Welsh Witch Company.
Wearing a witch's black hat, singer Stevie Nicks has been known
to dedicate songs during their concerts to "all the witches
of the world." She has been picked to play the title role
in a movie based on the myth of Rhiannon. (The album "Rumors"
was so popular it held the number one spot on the charts
for over six months and sold eight million copies.)

The black band Earth, Wind, and Fire has long explored
mysticism. Before going on stage, leader Maurice White (who
believes he possesses occult powers from previous incarnations)
has the entire group join hands in a circle to tune in the
force of "higher powers."[10] The very name of the group was
planned to encompass the elements: "wind" represents
their music and "fire" comes from White's astrological sign,
Sagittarius. His basis for faith was initiated by a study of
Buddhism resulting from his involvement in the martial arts.[11]
The big-selling album "All in All" features pictures of
Christian and occult symbols portrayed as synonymous in
authority and intent. Songs include "Serpentine Fire," about the
spinal life energy center taught in eastern religions.

Other popular rock artists whose music explores occult themes
include:

Todd Rundgren—his album "Ra" is dedicated to the Egyptian
sun god. The $250,000 stage for his band, Utopia, includes
a twenty-five-foot gold pyramid. Song lyrics are based on Japanese
and Egyptian mysticism.[12] Rundgren admits to believing in
astral projection and reincarnation.[13]

Stevie Wonder—his album "Songs in the Key of Life" was scheduled for a release to coincide with his astrological sign Taurus.[14]

Daryl Hall—like Jimmy Page, is a follower of Aleister Crowley. An admitted initiate of magic, he claims his song "Winged Bull" is dedicated to the ancient Celtic religion.[15]

Al Jardine—of the Beach Boys, has his astrology charts done to determine previous incarnations.[16]

America—recorded a song, "God of the Sun," about sun worship.[17]

Van Morrison—claims he has experienced a spiritual transformation as a result of reading literature on Celtic (witchcraft) history and the supernatural.[18]

Steve Hackett—guitarist for the group Genesis, recorded a solo album, "Voyage of the Acolyte," with songs based on his musical interpretation of the Tarot cards.

Jackson Browne—says his song "Rock Me on the Water" has mythological significance and declares, "Reincarnation is a certainty. It's a belief."[19]

Tangerine Dream—this group performed in a thirteen-century cathedral while smoking pot and urinating on the pillars. William Friedkin (director of *The Exorcist*) claims their music inspired his film *The Sorcerer*.[20]

Dr. John—wears voodoo necklaces and is an ordained minister in the Louisiana Church of Witchcraft.[21]

Cat Stevens—his interest in spiritualism has been expounded with the metaphysical imagery of "Katmandu" and "Moonshadow." Stevens is now a convert to Islam and spends his spare time in a mosque near his Rio home.

Meat Loaf—their album "Bat Out of Hell" features pictures of demons and tells of a mutant biker who rides out of the pit of Hell Composer Jim Steinman says, "I've always been fascinated by the supernatural and always felt rock was the perfect idiom for it."[22] The lead singer of Meat Loaf adds, "When I go on stage, I get possessed."[23]

Nazareth—released two albums ("Hair of the Dog" and "Expect No Mercy") with covers featuring demon manifestations that could only have been painted by an artist who had had spirit encounters. Another example of demonic art is found in the representations of Lucifer on Savoy Brown's "Hellbound Train."

Santana—their album "Abraxas" was named after a witchcraft demon.

Uriah Heep—an album entitled "Demons and Wizards" features a variety of occult songs such as "Traveler in Time" about astral projection.

Queen—the lyrics by lead singer Freddie Mercury in "Bohemian Rhapsody" declare that Beelzebub has a devil put aside for them.

David Bowie—purchased a record player to play records backwards because he believes songs of his "Young Americans" album resemble Tibetan spiritistic chants. At one point in his career reports had him drawing pentagrams on his walls and making hexes while candles burned.[24]

Heart—Ann and Nancy Wilson wrote a song called "Devil Delight" for the album "Magazine." They sing of sinister pleasures of a "dirty demon daughter."

Donna Summer—regularly rings up her astrologer for consultations and keeps an eye on the configurations of the heavens to arrange concerts and travel plans.[25]

Few groups could top the Rolling Stones for displays of blatant conjuring of evil. One of their early albums was entitled "Their Satanic Majesties Request." For the cover, they posed as witches. A Richard-Jagger composition "Sympathy for the Devil" has become an unofficial national anthem for Satanists. In this song, Lucifer himself speaks and requests "courtesy" and "sympathy" from all who meet him.

The ultimate Stones embodiment of dark images came on their album "Goat's Head Soup." Part of it was recorded at a Haitian voodoo ritual. Behind the music you can hear the screams of those who are becoming possessed of evil spirits. One song, "Dancing with Mr. D.," describes a graveyard romp with the devil himself. Inside the album is a color picture of a severed goat's head floating in a boiling cauldron. Surely the Stones are aware that the goat's head is the universal symbol of Satan worship.

After reading this chapter, let's suppose you discover your child has been listening to the music of these artists. Perhaps he even has their records in his own collection. Obviously, as a concerned parent you want to do something about it. You want your house to serve the Lord, and that desire will be seriously hindered if your children are exposed to music like this. What do you do?

Why not pose these questions to your children and pray that their response will lead them to make the right decision on their own?

QUESTION #1—Does the purchase of a record enhance that artist's popularity and, therefore, more widely disburse his philosophy?

When a rock artist is idolized by millions of impressionable minds, his outlook on the demonic may be more inviting because of his commercial success. It seems questionable whether any Christian young person would want his peers to experiment with the occult simply because his favorite rock star had recommended it.

QUESTION #2—If music has the ability to convey spiritual power as well as melodic and rhythmic content, what does this mean when a musician admits contact with the power of darkness?

Musical performers have the ability to invest in their art, to explore the power behind their creative impulses. In the biblical case of King David, we see that music can facilitate the presence of the Holy Spirit and hinder the work of evil spirits. Pagan rituals display the converse ability to conjure demons by rhythmic repetition and idolatrous devotion.

QUESTION #3—Is it really possible to listen to the music of a rock artist involved in the occult and appreciate his musicianship without being affected by either his lyrics or demonic inspiration?

Just as the anointing of the Holy Spirit may rest upon music that lifts the soul, Satan can also convey a counterfeit unction to create an unhealthy spiritual atmosphere. Whether or not the person listening to an occult-rock song is consciously listening to the words really makes no difference. The subconscious mind, the seat of the soul, is being affected.

QUESTION #4—When the record album of an artist involved in the occult is purchased, what are the implications of Christ's words in Matthew 12:30: "He that is not with me is against me"?

All occult phenomena come from Satan who is the enemy of God. Therefore, anyone who avows or advocates participation in such demonic practices has declared himself in opposition to the Lord. Should that person be aided in his cause by those who claim they are followers of Christ?

If your child answers these questions satisfactorily, a good bonfire may be in order. If the answers are disappointing, much prayer will certainly be necessary before he becomes a permanent resident of "Hotel California."

FOOTNOTES

[1]*Time*, August 15, 1975, p. 4.

[2]*Rolling Stone*, October 26, 1972, p. 12.

[3]*Rolling Stone*, December 16, 1976, p. 11.

[4]*Time*, December 16, 1974, p. 39.

[5]*Circus*, August 16, 1976, p. 30.

[6]*Ibid.*, June 22, 1978, p. 15.

[7]*Ibid.*, October 12, 1976, p. 41.

[8]*Ibid.*, March 17, 1977, p. 58.

[9]*Newsweek*, May 10, 1976, p. 121.

[10]*Circus*, January 19, 1977, p. 23.

[11]*Rolling Stone*, January 26, 1978, p. 14.

[12]*Billboard*, December 10, 1977, p. 38.

[13]*Circus*, November 1974, p. 64.

[14]*People*, July 19, 1976, p. 51.

[15]*Circus*, October 13, 1977, p. 28.

[16]*Ibid.*, May 26, 1977, p. 52.

[17]*Rolling Stone*, March 10, 1977, p. 27.

[18]*Ibid.*, July 1, 1976, p. 22.

[19]*Ibid.*, December 16, 1976, p. 61.

[20]*Ibid.*, August 28, 1975, p. 13.

[21]*Billboard*, October 12, 1974, p. 38.

[22]*Circus*, December 22, 1977, p. 12.

[23]*Time*, September 11, 1978.

[24]*Hit Parader*, July 1975, p. 16.

[25]*Ibid.*, December 4, 1978, p. 93.

SEVEN
SATURDAY NIGHT FEVER

"But we don't even touch when we dance. Why can't I go to the disco?"

At least you've got to admit they're right. But the fact that they don't touch somehow seems a small consolation. You are grateful that disco dancing doesn't seem to have the sensuous body contact that caused Christian parents to forbid such activity in your day. Still, inside you have the nagging feeling that today's dancing might actually, in some way, be even worse. If *Saturday Night Fever* has some morally questionable consequences, it's one disease you certainly don't want your children to catch.

Anyway, you're confused every time you hear that term "disco" used. You're not certain whether it's a place to go, something to do, a way to feel, or a sound to listen to. And watching those wildly atavistic dances they perform doesn't set your mind any more at ease. You begin to wonder if it isn't just old age setting in. "Maybe they are right," you surmise, "perhaps i don't understand kids these days."

Relax. Your confusion is warranted. Disco is a phenomenon that even some music industry experts don't understand. Its style and jargon are bound to be perplexing to any adult not tuned in to the exact wavelength of the youth culture. As for those gesticulatory maneuvers they call dancing, you have every right to be disturbed. But before we get into that, we'd better

clear the haze so that you at least understand where disco
came from and what it's doing to our world.

The word "disco" is a shortened form of the French word for
"record library," "discotheque." It was used in the late
sixties to describe rock nightclubs where the emphasis was on
dancing. (Remember go-go girls?) As we turned into the
seventies, discotheques went the way of hula hoops. The mood of
the decade just didn't fit "twisting the night away."

Vietnam and the sexual revolution sent the young on a search for
alternative life styles. The screams of Little Richard and
anarchic piano playing of Jerry Lee Lewis, to say nothing of the
pelvis of Elvis, ushered in a revolt against the Establishment.
Rock's nose-thumbing quality disdained those over thirty
and the success ethic of materialism. But disco has changed all
that.

The relentless beat of rock as characterized by disco has won its
way into the heart of mainstream America. Even moms and
dads are taking Hustle lessons while their wiggling children wile
away the weekends at kiddie discos. Conservative, respectable
businessmen are exchanging their button-down suits for
skin-tight flare pants and an orgy of gesticulatory pleasure. Disco
can now be heard in shopping centers, over the normally
somnambulant airwaves of Muzak, and in the best hotels. There
are disco proms, cruises, roller skating rinks, and even
a disco wedding service complete with smoke machines and
lighting effects.

It was the Bee Gees, John Travolta, and *Saturday Night Fever*
that set disco on fire. Disco invaded TV shows like "Don
Kirshner's Rock Concert" and "The Midnight Special." Radio
WKTU in New York turned its format from mellow rock to
disco and became the most listened-to station in the country. Such
far-flung artists as The Grateful Dead, Dolly Parton, and
the Beachboys went disco with astounding commercial success.
The Stones hit it big with their song, "Miss You," and
Rod Stewart vividly described a sensuous night of fornication
with his hit, "Do Ya Think I'm Sexy," and got the best selling
record of his career.

"But I still don't understand," you insist. "Telling me where it
came from and what it's doing still doesn't tell me what disco is."

Answering your question is like trying to define "soul."

When you hear it, you know it. When you've got it, you feel it. To confuse matters more, disco is used as an adjective, verb, and noun all in the same breath. Disco is not only what you do but also where you go.

It might help to explain that while all disco is rock, not all rock is disco. In other words, disco is a variant of rock music that uses a special facet of its beat and then embellishes it with characteristic arrangements. The sound of disco borrows from a diverse heritage fusing Latin rhythms with the black styles made popular by artists like James Brown and Sly Stone.

All disco has one thing in common: a sound that is manufactured to make you dance and dance and dance. The formula requires little creativity on the part of the individual session musician. In fact, the instrumentalist who goes into the studio to record a disco song may not even know on whose album he is playing. After laying down a basic drum, bass, and guitar track, the producer then calls in other musicians who subsequently stack on another thirty or forty tracks which are later remixed. It is the producer who must bring all the complex elements together, since only he may know what the final product is to sound like.

Whatever synthesizers, horns, vocals, or handclapping is tacked on, nothing is allowed to interfere with disco's relentless rhythm. The lyrics and melody are kept to a monotonous simplicity so that the unaccented regularity of the beat comes through. It must have, as one writer put it, "the imperative urgency of a war drum."[1] In fact, disco producers design their tunes to conform to a minimum of 125 beats per minute. Such metronome-like quality doesn't even require a real, live musician. For Donna Summer's hit, "I Feel Love," the drum sounds were created by an electronic sequencing device called a Drum Mate that simulates the sound of a snare and bass drum. Such concoctions may not be legitimately called music in a traditional sense, but the ultimate goal is to feel a sound, not hear it. As long as the hormones are induced to flow and the feet set to move, nothing else matters. Disco is a body trip, not a head trip, and shaking one's "booty" is what it's all about.

The dope and downers of the early seventies turned people inward. Most young people were looking inside their heads, and that left them little time to boogie with their bodies. Public

dancing was out and protest marching was in, except for a
dedicated minority of blacks and gays. In homosexual haunts,
dancing and drugs merged into a pharmaceutical fashion
show of glitter and decadence. For gays, disco became a rallying
cry to come out of the closet. They did, and today one
rock promoter estimates that 75 percent of all discos are gay-
operated. Undisputedly, almost all disco deejays and lighting
crews are gay, and homosexual patronage is considered a
must by the businessman who opens a new club.

Like most parents, you've probably never been to a disco. It's
another world you know nothing about, but one your
children may be asking to be part of. To spare you the trauma
of searching out your local disco, let's take a vicarious
journey inside those walls and see what goes on.

Inside, you encounter a fantasy world of mirrored walls, see-
through clothing, twirling glass balls, strobe lights, and
lasers as well as a pharmacopoeia of drugs. Poppers (amyl and butyl
nitrate), ethyl chloride, Quaaludes, and psychedelics fill
the heads of the dancers dressed in Lycra jeans and thigh-high-
split dresses. Periodically, the audience is showered in a
blizzard of white polyurethane (fake snow) to remind customers
that cocaine is their favorite drug because of the seemingly
boundless energy it produces. The purpose is to achieve an alert
body that's ready to do the "weekend two-step," "bionic
boogie," and "le freak." When we're finished here we could next
visit a roller disco where $200 skates are used to circumnambulate
the premises. Flashing lights and blaring music have replaced
the squeaky skates and organ solos you may remember.

What keeps disco going are the music and the deejays, the men
who play the music. There's more to the job than just slapping
another vinyl on the turntable. Some successful deejays
who easily earn $300 a night have developed their jobs into an art
form. With sound systems costing over $100,000, they
actually orchestrate the music by controlling the volume and
intensity of drum breaks as well as bass and string lines.
One prominent deejay memorizes the beats per minute of each
tune so he can ease the dancers out of one song into the
next. With the aid of laughing gas, pills, and pot, these alchemist
engineers pride themselves in being able to psyche out a
crowd into an ecstatic frenzy. One deejay admitted, "The drugs

(and music) really make the experience almost spiritual."

Now that you understand what disco is and where it is, hang on while we try to dispel a little more confusion. Just when you've started to cope with the names of the rock groups your kids want to listen to, along comes disco with an all-new roster of singers. Let's see who they are and what their music is saying.

Donna Summer reigns as disco's queen by virtue of a series of songs which qualify her for the title, First Lady of Lust. Known for her twisting pelvis and suggestive handling of the microphone during performances, she orgiastically groans that she needs some "hot stuff tonight." Although Donna insists on being accepted for talents beyond her physical endowments, her albums continue to display sensuous poses and lyrics designed to send male temperatures rising.

Chic claims their concept came from the rock group KISS, an attempt to do with disco what those white-faced, fire-breathers had done with their teen audiences. After seven years of traveling the Black chitlin club circuit, they finally hit it big with lyrical clichés like "Dance, Dance, Dance" and "Le Freak," which inspired an erotic dance. Bassist Bernard Edwards admits, "We make the group for the public. If tastes change, we will too."[2] Such expediency includes strong gay overtones and the admission that their "semi-decadent" image was designed for its commercial appeal.

The most outrageous of the successful disco artists is Sylvester, an avowed transvestite whose stage costuming is drag-queen regalia. The Mayor of San Francisco proclaimed a day in his honor, and his albums earn gold records. In spite of his gender-bending ways, Sylvester admits that his professional singing career started on the California gospel circuit.

The biggest disco group is comprised of five gays and one straight who call themselves the Village People. They come onstage decked out as a hard hat, an Indian, a cowboy, a policeman, a GI, and a homosexual leather freak. Their manager, Jaques Morali (who himself is a publicly acknowledged homosexual), admits he formed the group as a "protest against Anita Bryant." Morali declares, "I am sincerely trying to produce songs to make the gay people more acceptable."[3] Twelve million people have bought their records with tunes like "Y.M.C.A.," a paean of praise to homosexuality that describes

the titled designation as a place where you can "hang out
with all the boys" and find many ways to have a "good time." One
album, "Cruising," is named after the homosexual practice
of driving around to spot other gays who can be propositioned. In
spite of their depraved antics, Merv Griffin featured them
for ninety minutes on nation-wide television, and the U.S. Navy
has considered adopting their hit, "In the Navy," for its
recruiting program.

Obviously, if your children want to make it in the disco scene,
they have some serious questions to consider. The blatant
homosexual advocacy and emphasis on promiscuity that are part
of disco mark its moral philosophies as forbidden territory
for the committed Christian. This is not to suggest that everything
about disco is vile and depraved, but some categoric conclusions
can be drawn by this survey of its songs and life styles.

Once you have convinced your children that most of the disco
songs and singers are off-limits, there is still the issue of
dancing to be resolved. You can't bring up the old objection
regarding illicit arousal of passions resulting from prolonged
physical contact. Remember the argument, "We don't even
touch."

If your children are honest, they'll admit that contention may
be partly true, but hardly a worthy defense. Take, for
example, one of the more popular disco dances, "Le Freak." The
partners crouch with knees bent and legs spread and proceed
to thrust their pelvises against each other in time to the music. In
one city, two jealous males were driven to murder after
watching their dates spend the evening "freaking" with other
men. Other dance routines require that the bodies meet on
a collision course with various parts of the anatomy banging into
one's partner. The male ungracefully flings his mate about,
slamming against her with more than gentle vigor. The naive
teenager may find it all great fun, but the gays in the crowd will
readily recognize the sadomasochistic flavor of such exhibitions.

Citing such extreme examples may keep your children off
the disco floor for a while, but a more comprehensive understanding of dancing will be needed if they are to develop a
rational Christian perspective on the subject. To do that, it will be
necessary to discover where dancing came from and what its
meaning is in modern society.

Who was the first dancer? It may have been Satan. As the first created musician, he may have expressed his exuberance by dancing around the throne of God. After Satan fell, perhaps he determined his "talent" for dancing would be a major means of corrupting mankind. He could take what God intended as a way of integrating the body and emotions in a form of worship and corrupt it into a sensuous display of erotic behavior. Though the Old Testament recounts instances when God's people danced to convey their joy and praise, history shows that pagan societies first connected dancing with courtship, puberty, and fertility rites. Even the Israelites were subject to such base impulses, as shown by the degeneration of their musical expressions. Compare their conduct following the Red Sea deliverance (Ex. 15) with their sinful festivity about the golden calf (Ex. 32).

The *Encyclopedia Americana* says of dancing: "In summation, it may be said that primitive man—yesterday and today—found his reason for dancing in religion or magic, in his own physical energy, in sexual drives, and in the need to communicate; and modern man, if he pauses for analysis, will find these ancient sources provide the stimuli for all of his dances, folk or theatrical, to this day."[4]

Agnes de Mille, a well-known dancer and choreographer, has this to say in her book, *The Book of the Dance:*

It is in the history of mating dances that we must look for a possible explanation of the extraordinary atavistic performances preferred by our young today. It is no accident that they carry on the way they do. When courtship dances are courteous, done with grace and decorum and to a pattern, they represent a step forward in man's slow progress toward relationship. When they are rough and graceless, they reflect a disintegration not only of individuals but of community life as well. The more primitive the people, the more distant to each other. . . . The partners tend to keep separate, not touching. . . . They jig on in a kind of self-hypnosis; . . . a dance floor today is not a group of couples but a crowd of individuals moving in concert. The individual . . . is a separate figure working entirely on his own without plan. This, as far as I know, has never occurred before.[5]

"They don't even touch?" In the light of secular comments like this, such justifications lose some of their luster. The reason

for not touching is to allow more bodily freedom so that there are
no restrictions on gesticulatory movements. Footwork and
grace are not the focus of expression. In plain language, erotic
manipulations pertaining to the shoulders, breasts, hips,
and genitals is what dancing today is all about. No less an
unexpected source than Mick Jagger of the Rolling Stones
declared, "All dancing is a replacement for sex."[6]

Mr. Jagger's opinion is buttressed by the more academic view
of Dr. Franzblau, a noted New York psychiatrist, who has
observed, "Many of these dances are really the modern version of
the tribal dances, and dancing is body language.... Of
course, many of these dances... may be a way of wooing and
courting, the foreplay to lovemaking."

If your children aren't convinced by now that the erotic
maneuvers of modern male-female dance techniques represent
questionable Christian conduct, here is one more suggestion. Ask
them if they'd be willing to give an illustration of their
dancing abilities in a suitable public setting. After all, the disco
is a place where their bodily contortions can be viewed
indiscriminately. What would be wrong with doing the same thing
on your church platform?

I doubt they'd accept the challenge. Could this mean that they
support a double set of standards? Is the injunction of
1 Corinthians 6:19, 20 to treat our bodies as the temple of God's
Spirit applied differently when one is in God's house as
compared to in the disco?

Once the point has been driven home, don't be too hard on your
children. The sexual overtones of disco dancing that may
be so obvious to you may honestly not be apparent to them.
Christian teenagers tend to be somewhat transparent regarding
the full range of sexual expressions and stimulation. They
may assume that an understanding of the anatomical aspects of sex
qualifies them to evaluate those circumstances which can
stir unhealthy desires. Thus, they run the risk of failing to
recognize more subtle forms of sexually related behavior.

Your children may see disco dancing as a harmless form of
physical pleasure, a way to let off steam, or a time for congregating
with friends who enjoy a good time. As they move to the
music, their main conscious attention is focused on the mere
physical skills of participating in the dance movements.

But unconsciously, these manipulations are sending a clear
message: The human body is foremost an object of sexual pleasure,
and the excitation of basic drives need not be restricted
to the private quarters of the matrimonial bed. Those who have a
scriptural respect for the beauty of sexual conduct in marriage
will understand why it is so important that the body God
gave us not be bartered promiscuously at a disco where the music
and movements are usually programmed with an erotic intention.

Now that you understand disco as music and disco as
dancing, we need to place this musical phenomenon into an
overall spiritual perspective.

Dance crazes and music styles come and go with the ebb and
flow of popular culture's response to whatever hedonistic impulses
may be prevailing. Disco may soon fade from the scene to
the graveyard of the Jitter-Bug and Lindy-Hop. But why has it so
captivated a large percentage of the present populace?

Neil Bogart, head of Casablanca Records (a major disco label),
says, "If I can, through [disco], create a fantasy for people,
give them a couple of hours with which they can dance to make
them forget. . .then I think I'm doing a public service."[7]
Rock critic Robert Hilburn adds, "Disco is a temporary thrill—a
night in a bordello."[8] Another writer calls it "the music
that fiddles while Rome burns."[9]

Disco is an outgrowth of Western man's three current pre-
occupations: sex, success, and cynicism. Nothing matters
more than the physical pleasure of the body and indulging in
whatever sensory stimulation the material accomplishments of
affluence can provide. Underneath such cravings, an almost
narcissistic attitude prevails. "Everyone's a winner," one disco
song declares, and it might be added, on the dance floor,
everyone's a superstar. "Love thyself" is disco's foremost social
ethic. "If it feels good, don't hold back," declares a recent
disco hit.

The environment at a disco is designed to induce a drug-like
state with the mesmerizing influence of the lights, the beat, and
the fantasized atmosphere. The neurosensory responses are
overloaded until the dancers project their minds to an escapist
level of oblivion. In such a stupefied state, the realities
of life and the guilt of sin are negated with the same mind-altering
intensity associated with hallucinogens or transcendentalism.

The impulse for this kind of indulgence was perhaps best expressed by Patti Labelle's disco hit, "Music Is My Way of Life." Patti laments that there's nothing to live for in her world. She declares that dancing is her only way out, the time when she gets to live her fantasies.

But fairy tales are, after all, not true. Sooner or later the turntables stop and the lights fade. Beyond the doors of the disco, a hostile world controlled by evil forces awaits the dancers who must come down and walk out. The would-be John Travoltas and the disco Cinderellas are suddenly thrust into real life where there are real and perplexing problems that can't be cured by shaking one's booty. When the skin-tight trousers and see-through dresses are hung up, the lonely silence of sin's consequences closes in. A few pills will enforce the slumber of sleep, but tomorrow will be another day to endure until Saturday Night Fever strikes again.

FOOTNOTES

[1]*Newsweek*, April 2, 1979.

[2]*Ibid.*

[3]*Ibid.*

[4]*Encyclopedia Americana*, Vol. 8, 1965, p. 447.

[5]*New York Times Magazine*, October 27, 1965, pp. 30-31, 104.

[6]*G. Q. Scene*, Spring, 1967, p. 72.

[7]*Rolling Stone*, April 19, 1979, p. 41.

[8]*Newsweek*, April 2, 1979.

[9]*Ibid.*

EIGHT
EVERYBODY DOES IT

Shocked, aren't you? The rock scene may have seemed offensive, but you never heard such specific and explicit explanations of why. If you as a parent are a little shook up, at least your awareness has been jarred. Now you see as never before the need for some musical standards to be established in your home.

But wait! Don't grab that hammer and charge into your children's rooms to break up all their rock albums. In the first place you might break some perfectly harmless records that will only convince them of your lunacy. Let's suppose you do find (or have found) some objectionable records in their collection. You allowed them to be bought in the first place, so don't become suddenly self-righteous. Breaking that record may also destroy any lines of communication between you that are still left open.

What you need to understand is that the record you now see to be so dangerous to your children's spiritual welfare is a symptom, not the problem. Destroying the effect won't make the cause go away.

After reading this far, you should be convinced that much of the rock scene is morally questionable at best and filled with perversion and debauchery at the worst. I know what you're thinking, "How could my children tolerate such filth invading their minds day after day?"

Unfortunately, most moms and dads ask that question as if it represents a personal threat to their success as parents. Now that you know what those songs and singers are really all about, you're probably horrified to think that after all you've done to properly train your children, they may still violate the principles you hoped to instill.

Parent, take the knife away from your throat. You haven't failed. You have just underestimated the power of today's culture to induce conformity. Why does your decent Sunday-school-bred boy wear a Foghat T-shirt and need to be herded to the barber under threat of dire punishment? The answer is simple—peer pressure.

It's too bad you can't spend a day at school with your children and listen to the content of their friends' conversations. In your generation kids talked about baseball stars and matinee idols. Today, it's rock songs and singers who provide the major topic.

When the majority of the other students know the words and tune to every hit on the charts, imagine how out of place your children would feel if they didn't. It's an understood norm of the youth culture. "Everybody" listens to rock. Your children know that if they aren't aware of the latest album by KISS, the most recent sleeping partner of David Bowie, and the much publicized drug bust of their favorite dope-rock group, they haven't got much to discuss with their peers.

Don't ever take too lightly the "everybody does it" syndrome. Everybody may not do it, but if your children think that, it's all the same to them. The irony is that your children most likely want to be nonconformist and yet end up conforming to the nonconformity of their culture. That's why your son puts on his tattered blue jeans, grows his hair shoulder-length, and takes off to a Queen concert looking like an exact replica of the other 10,000 kids there. You can see right through the conformity of his nonconformity, but he can't.

Ours is an age of depersonalization. This generation is tired of being treated like a number on a computer card. They want an identity that stands apart from the norm. And since adults establish the criteria for acceptance by the majority of society, rebelling against middle-class values is one way of saying, "You'll have to notice me because I'm different." Different from each other? No, but different from what their rock stars tell them is a corrupt, plastic generation of their elders.

Coupled with the desire for identity is the craving for acceptance. Admit it. You need it as much as your children do. Where do you get it? From social clubs, business associates, and organized institutions. Most of all, you find acceptance in your marriage partner, the one with whom you share your deepest fears and hopes. None of these options is readily open to the teenager, especially the latter.

Add to this the sexual pressures of modern life. Nearly every product advertised has subtle or overt implications that its use insures attraction to the opposite sex. Male-female relationships provide the ultimate means of indicating acceptance. Put yourself in the position of your children. If they violate the norm of being tuned in and turned on to the world of rock, what potential partners would look their way? Wouldn't such a deviation indicate that your children are really some kind of weirdos?

This is not to suggest or condone a permissive attitude toward the standards with which your child is confronted. Carnal desires on his part cannot be excused. A Christian teenager shouldn't want to attend a Jefferson Starship concert, and Christian parents shouldn't permit it; but the purpose of this chapter is to explain the peer pressures of adolescent conformity, not the idealistic desires of parents.

With all of the world arrayed against you and the power of the rock culture poised to devour your children's values, what is a parent to do? For one thing, be sympathetic to young people's problems and pressures. Don't overreact to the faddish influences in their lives. You've got your wife or husband to talk things over with. But remember, your children are being convinced by their culture that only the Knack and the Cars really understand what they are going through in the throes of adolescence.

Don't try to fight the norms of the rock culture head on. I may be able to give public lectures refuting the depraved ideologies of today's rock stars. But I have three things going for me that you may not: my background as an entertainer, my age, and my researched knowledge. I probably know more about the rock scene than most teenagers do, so they have to listen to me. You are not likely to have these kinds of advantages.

Don't worry. God has given you something I don't have. The Lord has placed an inbred, intuitive respect in your children for the parents who raised them. They may fight harder with you, but underneath they know you're really doing what you think is best. You don't have to know every song and singer on the charts to point out the obvious spiritual deficiencies in their lives and to question your children's identification with that kind of a life style.

Above all, don't release your frustrations in a torrent of anger. Let's suppose your children have become caught up in the rock culture. Should you burn your son's Alice Cooper T-shirt and insist he get an immediate crew cut? You can, but the cure might turn out to be worse than the cause.

A friend of ours woke up one day to find her twelve-year-old daughter had papered an entire wall with pictures of Shaun Cassidy. She asked my opinion. I told her that I felt such pre-puberty fascination with rock-sex idols was unhealthy. Directing her attention to the pictures her child had displayed, I pointed out Cassidy's half-bared chest, tight pants with appropriate bulges, and sexy gazes and poses.

"You should see what a Shaun Cassidy concert is like," I explained. "He suggestively dangles the microphone between his legs and caresses his bottom while he sings. Toward the end he takes off his trousers. Fortunately, he has on an even tighter pair underneath."

The mother blushed for a moment at such an explicit admission of the motives behind pre-teen rock performers. But she kept her cool and resisted the temptation to rip every picture from the wall with righteous anger. She decided to surreptitiously take down one picture a day while at the same time replacing them with more appropriate posters and pictures.

Another way to combat peer pressure is to provide contrasting role models within the Christian community. Point your children to pastors, evangelists, writers, and musicians who are understanding of society's trends and yet resist the tendency to completely emulate secular culture. I've often remarked that the greatest impact of my own ministry is through my life, not my sermons. If my wife and I can present before young people the positive image of a couple who love God and each other, we'll do more to influence their value judgments than any amount of preaching could ever accomplish.

Remember what I said at the beginning of this chapter? The affinity your children have for immoral rock songs and singers is a symptom. Getting them to put those kinds of records aside and develop more discerning musical tastes won't be easy. Nothing would please you more than to have them make a clean break with this kind of music, but the peer pressure may be too great for them to accomplish such a drastic change in their values overnight. You can pray for a gradual process of spiritual enlightenment on their part. This book will show you how that can be achieved.

NINE
THE BEAT GOES ON

It's been a long day but at last you have a few moments to
yourself. The dishes are done, the dog's been fed, and you've only
got two chapters left in that new book you've been reading.
Your husband, George, is absorbed with the football game on TV,
so attempting conversation is pointless. This is your time
of the day. Nothing to bug you. Just a few minutes of peace and
quiet.

You've only gotten about three pages into chapter ten when . . .
THUMP—THUMP. It sounds as if the roof is caving in, but
you know better. Your daughter's bedroom is directly above you,
and she is supposed to be doing homework. But how can
she concentrate? Why, you can't even hear the melody line, let
alone the words. They vaguely come through as a barely
audible series of screams and groans. But one thing does come
through, that THUMP—THUMP.

You try to ignore it, but the beat goes on. Why can't she listen
to some soft and pretty music—the kind that you enjoy?
At least her mind would be more settled to do algebra equations.
That isn't even music. It's only a THUMP—THUMP—and
your patience just can't take it any longer.

"George, do you hear what your daughter is doing? No wonder
she gets C's all the time. That beat is driving her crazy. She'll just
have to turn the stereo off."

"Uh huh," George replies. Obviously, fourth down on the
one-yard line is more important to him.

"Right now, George! You've got to do something."

"Uh huh."

It's no use. George isn't going to respond. You'll have to take matters into your own hands and stop that THUMP—THUMP once and for all.

Resolutely laying your book down, you head for your daughter's bedroom. Up the stairs and to her door. No need to worry that she'll hear you coming. That THUMP—THUMP drowns out everything.

You open the door. She's seated at the desk with her back to you. Bouncing up and down in the chair, she occasionally makes a mark with her pencil. She is doing homework, but how, you'll never know. There's the stereo and there's the plug. Pull it and you'll have tranquility restored to your home.

But before you yank the cord from the wall to silence your daughter's records, stop to consider a couple of things. Does pulling that plug now mean she won't listen to that music somewhere else later? Wouldn't it be better if your daughter understood for herself what some rock music can do to her mind, and abstained of her own free will?

Please remember that you were the one who allowed those records in your home in the first place. What if your sudden, heavy hand of discipline creates rebellion rather than submission? Wouldn't it be wise to find out why your daughter likes that music?

We've already discussed the role that peer pressure plays in turning kids on to rock. But that kind of influence is external. What about the internal craving for rock's beat that seems to inhabit nearly every teen in today's rock generation? I know how offensive and nerve-wracking that driving, throbbing beat of rock is to your sensibilities, but believe it or not, kids really like it.

Now before we look into why young people develop such an affinity for the rhythm of rock, let's make certain that we have a definitive understanding as to what rock is and how it is musically constructed. The reason for this is vital. First of all, parents who merely find the beat irritating may fail to comprehend the power it has to captivate the body and mind, making the latter susceptible to the message of the music.

Parents who want to relate to their children with a reasonably perceptive understanding of the rock scene need first of all to get their terminology straight. I'm not trying to be overly technical about this matter. It's just that I know how kids think.

When you try to discuss the issue of music, they're on the defensive anyway. They're looking for a semantic blunder on your part that will disqualify anything else you say about their musical tastes. Calling Elton John hard rock (he's not) or assuming that every freaky looking group lays down primitive, unsophisticated beat patterns (e.g., Electric Light Orchestra does not) may be the mortal sin that turns off all communication.

It's also important for you as a parent to realize that just because the music may not sound like Lawrence Welk, the rhythms aren't necessarily objectionable or even classifiable as rock. So, as a help to the parent who's ready to pull the plug on the stereo, let's explore the world of rock's rhythms and find out where some lines can be drawn in your child's musical diet.

Many parents are confused as to the differences between "rock" and "rock and roll." At first the term rock was only an abbreviated form of rock and roll. In the last few years, however, a chronological and musical distinction between the terms has evolved. Though both are still used somewhat interchangeably, rock and roll refers primarily to pre-1964 music or present-day music which emulates the style of artists such as Little Richard, Elvis, Bill Haley, Chuck Berry, and early Beach Boys. It was played mainly by blacks who used pianos and horns, whereas today's rock is performed mostly by whites in small bands with the guitar predominant. Musically, rock and roll is a primitive, loud, and driving musical form which provided the root for hard rock.

The broadened term of rock came into journalist vogue in the late sixties and refers primarily to post-Beatle music. Its definition is less precise and may include the work of such diverse artists as Billy Joel and Eric Clapton. Rock is a music of greater surface seriousness and lyrical complexity than rock and roll. As the product of self-aware musicians, rock is a more middle-class music than its predecessor. However, the terms "rock" and "rock and roll" are often used interchangeably by both musicians and the record-buying public.

The instrument most closely associated with rock is the guitar. From its conception, this has been the basic sound, primarily because of its rhythmic quality. Although the unamplified acoustic guitar finds its way into some of the softer forms of rock, the electric guitar is still used the most.

Taking their cue from country and western music, the first groups utilized four basic instruments: two guitars for lead and rhythm, a bass, and drums. Toward the end of the fifties, other instruments were added to the ensemble. Pianos and saxophones soon became popular, and the dawn of the sixties reverberated with a variety of sounds from rock bands.

Brass ensembles and string sections with elaborate vocal backing introduced new possibilities. For the first time full orchestras began performing rock music. Then late in 1963 the Beatles appeared and started a trend back to small combos with the guitar as the basic sound once again.

During the sixties there were several brief detours into electronic and orchestral sophistication, but the four- or five-piece rhythm unit predominated. Since rock is the hybrid sound of whole traditions of music (jazz, black spirituals, country and western, blues), it is hard to assign any one sound as typical. It has become a musical melting pot for many styles, all centered in the relentless beat.

Despite the variations and transitions, the essence of rock—the beat—has never been lost. Whatever harmonic or melodic or verbal sophistication rock may contain, it would never appeal as it does without the undergirding of its simple, rhythmic, pounding beat.

Mark Farner, lead guitarist for the now-disbanded Grand Funk rock group, expressed it this way: "I think that now the beat of rock and roll has been driven in. I think that as long as that beat, that feeling, is there—it might not be called rock and roll ten years from now—but it'll be there. That feeling will be there."

Any song can be constructed and performed with a rock format. One aspect of the term "rock" refers to a beat pattern that is incessant and repetitive. This is done by pulsating or syncopating the rhythm line.

Pulsation is the rhythmic, driving sound most easily associated with rock. It was originally introduced in the early sixties as the West Cost Surfing Sound and consisted of a rapid, throbbing beat. The first pulsation emphasis was upon the guitar and was generated by strumming with a pick on the lower strings with a successive striking manner. As use of the electric bass rose in influence, it intensified the pulsation of the rhythm guitar and percussion. In more recent years the blues and soul influences have caused the pulsation to be much slower in tempo.

A slowed pulsation is usually associated with a "heavy" sound. "Heavy" is a slang adjective which can mean that something is fine, good, or great, or it can be used in describing rock (heavy rock). Not all rock is heavy. It is, however, the most basic of the rock sounds and the one most directly related to the rock-and-roll era. It is heavy in that it trumpets in your ear like a herd of charging elephants. The beat is relentless, and it attacks and weighs on your senses with a driving insistence.

An incessantly driving, pulsated beat pattern is not inherently evil, but when applied for a protracted period of time at a high volume level, its spiritual effect can be devastating, especially at live concerts. Like any repetitious assault on one's neurosensory apparatus, it may shut down the conscious mental processes. This is the same technique used in eastern meditative disciplines such as Transcendental Meditation. The result is an inroad to the mind open for evil invasion.

If a particular song has a musical pulsation somewhere in its structure, that does not mean it has a negative spiritual potential. But if that pulsation is loud and long enough, it may induce a mindset whereby the hearer has surrendered his volitional authority. This is especially true in the case of the heavier rock groups whose live performances can rhythmically manipulate an audience until they reach a zombie-like state. In that condition, their minds are nonobjectively open to the message of the music, and their bodies are possible prey to evil spirits that readily operate through such entrancing music.

While spiritual devastation may be possible with a pulsated beat, erotic stimulation is sometimes the offspring of a syncopated rhythm. With syncopation, the accent is placed on the off beat in 4/4 time, as compared with other forms of music that accent the first and third beats. Syncopated rhythms can evoke sensuous response from the human body, particularly when they are electronically accentuated. This is because many of the vital processes of life are based upon rhythm. The vascular, respiratory, and autonomic nervous systems all use it to perform their functions. Man, therefore, has an inherent affinity for, and response to, certain rhythms.

This does not mean that pulsation and syncopation are immoral

rhythms. The major concern from a spiritual standpoint
is the extent to which the beat overrides all other musical elements
in a song so that the basic level of communication is sexually
and physically captivating. In fact, some of the more erotic secular
rock bands deliberately try to "turn on" an audience in this way.

If rhythms are not evil per se, how can they eroticize an
audience? This may depend upon many subjective criteria such as
the moral climate, the volume level of the performance,
the motive of the artist, the length of the production, and whether
the listener or dancer is sensuously inclined. There are no
definitive guidelines with which to gauge the moral effect of any
kind of music. This is a matter that must be judged on a
personal basis that takes into account all the variables involved.

Some people automatically designate any pulsated or
syncopated rhythm as morally dangerous, while others excuse all
rhythms with transparent naiveté. Both positions are
debatable, and neither contributes to an understanding of the
problems found in the rock idiom.

The focus of rock is usually on the beat. It is a drummer's
holiday. Such is the impact of the percussion section that, for
example, the drummer for one popular rock group beat his
drums so hard during performances that doctors ordered his hands
bandaged to prevent bleeding. I have known of hard rock
drummers who have admitted to having self-induced orgasms
after several hours of incessant drumming.

Jazz has a rhythmic swing. It flows with an exciting, yet
ultimately releasing feeling. But heavy rock is built from
a hard, straight-up-and-down pounding rhythm that produces
frustrated energy. Some rock sounds emphasize alternating
beats, while other rock tunes, in part or whole, hammer every
beat home. Though he may add fills (short percussion
outbursts), it is the drummer's job to keep the force of rock moving
with the incessant pulsating or syncopated beat.

The hearer must be enveloped in sound, immersed in the
overpowering effect of rock's electronic assault. Rock, at least in
its harsher forms, doesn't tickle your ears. It jams you in
the skull like a freight train. You don't listen to hard rock; it
baptizes you with a liturgy of sex, drugs, perversion, and the
occult. And because of the captivating power of the medium, it is
hard to objectify the message.

Now, Mom and Dad, do you understand why your child is so caught up in the beat of that music? It's not just noise but a carefully constructed means of captivating their bodies and capturing their minds. Because of the high-energy world in which you are raising them, they have developed a physiological affinity for that beat.

I know it drives you up the wall and sets your nerves on edge. But they really like it. The same rhythms that repel you, compel them. And because of the addictive nature of rock's rhythm, they can't be easily weaned away. The beat of rock may be potentially destructive under highly selective circumstances (e.g., when accompanied by drug usage, when performed at an ear-damaging decibel level at live concerts, when used as a mind-expanding or entrancing tool by occultic rock groups). But your main concern should be directed toward what the lyrics say and the singers do.

Don't get too hung up on the beat of rock. Its musical form is not your biggest problem, but you need to understand that driving sound for the way in which it envelopes the world your child lives in. He may move to the sound of a different drummer, and no matter how much you detest it, he may like it. Don't mock it or knock it. That won't get you anywhere. That beat must be replaced by something better suited to healthy moral and musical development.

TEN
DO AS I SAY—AND AS I DO

So far we've explored how your child is pressured and cajoled
into an identification with the rock culture. Now, we come
to the hard part of the book: putting you, Mom and Dad, on the
spot.

Perhaps you've already tried with little success to discipline
your child's musical habits. He just wouldn't listen to what
you said. Is it possible that your failure was due to a lack of moral
authority? Does what you *say* contradict what you *do?*

There's no way to drop it on you gently. One of the main reasons
children fail to respond to instructions regarding musical
standards is the inconsistency of parental examples. In short,
adult hypocrisy, not a rock conspiracy, may turn kids off
to Mom and Dad and on to Cheap Trick.

Whenever I challenge teenagers to use discrimination in the
secular music world, they immediately retort with two
arguments: "What about the TV programs my parents watch?" or
"The music they listen to isn't much better."

What about it, Mom and Dad? Is your example an asset or a
detriment? Are you willing to be honest with yourselves
and with your children? Let's take a hard look at some adult
hypocrisies that only serve to drive teenagers deeper into
the rock culture.

One of the main arguments against a teen's absorption of the
rock culture is based on his frequency of contact with its value

system. As a parent, you could probably overlook the depravity of some rock if it were only an occasional or passing interest in the life of your child. It isn't. He listens to it constantly. He wakes up to rock on the clock radio, dresses and eats breakfast to it, listens to it on the car radio going to school, takes the transistor with him during the day, and at night does his homework with the stereo blaring until he finally drops off to sleep with a transistor under his pillow.

Nothing has more pervasive contact with his life, and that's what bothers you. But try to confront him about it, and he immediately brings up the multiplied hours you spend in front of the TV. Just as you think he's been propagandized by the Rolling Stones, he sees you as having been brainwashed by "The Edge of Night," and "Charlie's Angels."

This indoctrination begins right in the living room where TV's cesspool drops the devil's garbage into the family circle. Put yourself in the place of a TV show writer. Programming's voracious appetite for new ideas has long ago reached the satiation point. What is left but to explore the forbidden boundaries of sex and violence? The glorification of the sensual has gone beyond adultery to incest and homosexuality, with the subtle intent of reeducating America's morality.

The proliferation of crime shows based on murder and mayhem is schooling many people in criminally insane values. In some cities today the hand that once reached for candy now holds out a "Saturday Night Special" and threatens your pocketbook. The youngster may have learned the intricacies of villainy via "Hawaii Five-O" and "Kojak."

One evening as I sat on my front porch reading, I overheard the conversation of several neighborhood kids. "It's my turn to commit a crime," one of them called out to his playacting friend. "This time I get to kill somebody."

Of course, most Christian parents don't attend X-rated movies. They don't need to. Why waste the money when they can wait two years and digest the same lascivious fare in the comfort of their own living room? A single program may not warp one's mind, but the average high school graduate has spent more time watching TV (about 14,000 hours) than he has spent in school (little more than 10,000) or church. It is this insistent bombardment of concepts contrary to Christian values that may eventually recondition his morality.

If the garbage of TV's audiovisual debauchery has a waste dump, it's the afternoon—Mom's prime time to turn on to her vicarious fantasies of love American style. It should be obvious that the soap operas are an insidious assault on Christian standards through the morally reprehensible themes they portray. But let me be more specific and list some reasons for Christians to object to the soaps:

(1) *The life styles presented as normal are, in fact, the warped concoctions of Hollywood and New York writers who project their own perversions as common fare for the American housewife.*

Women are wicked and men are manipulative, according to the soap portrayal of the "average" household. Do you really know any family that could sustain five affairs, four abortions, three seductions, two suicides, and one attempted case of incest—all in one year? Do you long to cheat on your husband, suspect him of sleeping with his secretary, expect to have your teenage daughter turn up pregnant, and depressively desire to slit your wrists in sheer frustration? If so, the soaps fairly well represent your life. If not, then why subject your mind to questionable dramas that proficiently portray a generation doomed for hell?

(2) *There is an overpowering urge to identify with the characters conveyed in the soaps.*

Viewers cry, laugh, and copy each emotional trauma as if the actors were real people. What is pure make-believe has become reality for soap addicts. They have been known to send CARE packages to poor soap characters and have bought clothes and champagne to celebrate fictitious weddings. One actress, whose role included a mastectomy resulting from breast cancer, was deluged in real life by letters of condolence. Such empathizing may find one rationalizing sin and sympathizing with the harried wife who seeks solace in seduction. "After all," you may find yourself saying, "that tormenting husband drove her to it." Don't underestimate the power of drama to involve the observer morally as well as emotionally.

(3) *What you have seen portrayed on TV may not seem nearly as repulsive in real life once you have been thoroughly indoctrinated.*

The soaps are trendsetters for America's moral attitude toward life and love. After months of seeing unbridled lust extolled each afternoon, the most unsuspecting mother may be a willing candidate for adultery. If the habits of teens are established by the rock stars they worship, the middle-aged matrons of America who idolize the soap characters are equally idolatrous toward their matinee heroes who survive by deceit and fornication.

Perhaps you think such language is a little too pointed. Couldn't the matter have been discussed a little more gently? Perhaps. But the situation is serious, and major surgery is in order. You're concerned about the music your children are listening to. If one reason is your hypocritical standards toward the TV programs you watch, the point needs to be forcibly brought home.

You may argue that one person can't control what the networks show. But we're all to blame. Manufacturers only advertise on TV programs with an audience, and any boycott must begin at the consumer market level to be effective. Are not Christians supposed to be the preservative of society, the "salt of the earth" (Matt. 5:13)? Can we then contribute with a clear conscience to the rotten viewing habits of millions who don't know the Lord? What about our responsibility to "redeem the time" (Eph. 5:16)? While souls are seeking for love and a purpose in life, some Christians are more concerned about "The Young and Restless" and "The Days of Our Lives."

Try this experiment. For one week's average viewing diet, make a list of how many times you are subjected to the following: (1) profanity, (2) the Lord's name used in vain, (3) adultery and fornication portrayed or suggested, (4) murders or attempted murders, (5) assaults (verbal and physical), (6) favorable attitudes toward homosexuality, (7) cheating and corner-cutting to get ahead, (8) dirty jokes and lewd remarks, (9) Christianity mocked or attacked, and (10) occult practices glorified or used to instill horror.

You may be appalled at the contents of your list. Next, show that list to your child and tell him what you plan to do about it. (Hopefully, your decision will be to carefully monitor the future viewing habits in your home.) Ask your child to follow your example. From the music he normally listens to, and the rock stars he usually identifies with, have him make his own list. With much prayer, that list and your example should start to solve the problem of rock music's influence on the life of your child.

ELEVEN
WHAT IS A PARENT TO DO?

Perhaps this book was intended for your family. You see your children and your lives portrayed on its pages. Furthermore, you understand the first premise of chapter one: your child's involvement in the rock scene is a symptom as well as a problem. Now, what are you to do?

Raising your children in the rock generation will require the understanding of Solomon and the honesty of David. The former was endowed by God with supernatural perception. In the New Testament, James 1:5 promises you the same wisdom. David was not only a man who failed, but also one who acknowledged his shortcomings. Your readiness to do the same will be an important factor in gaining back the respect from your child which you may have lost.

Specifically, there are three steps you can take immediately to establish lines of communication with your children. They are:

(1) Be informed.
(2) Show love.
(3) Set an example.

Part of your shock at reading about the depravity in the rock scene was due to lack of information. It's surprising how little most parents know about the world of music their children live in. I have stood outside rock concert halls and watched car after car drive up to disgorge its teenage occupants. "Have a good time," Mom says as she drives away, leaving her thirteen-year-old daughter to indulge in an evening of drugs and the titillation of sexual invitations.

The average rock concert is a law-free zone of drug usage. The atmosphere is so saturated with euphoric odors that one deep breath is sometimes enough to get high. Before the first song is ever played, out will come the pipes from the jeans pockets. Those who don't come supplied with their own plastic bag full of goodies can easily borrow from a friend. The band onstage yells at the crowd, "Get high. Toke a joint and groove with the sounds."

Getting stoned on dope is the norm at most rock fests and concerts. With no hassles from the cops to worry about and two hours of high-energy music to look forward to, tripping out is part of the reason for going in the first place. What do the authorities do? Nothing. To arrest any number of drug offenders would start a riot with serious injuries. Anyway, what do you do with 5,000 kids after you've arrested them? Just imagine the wrath of most parents who are certain that their child doesn't use drugs and who think the police must be in error.

Why don't more parents know what's going on? Don't they read the papers? Can't they smell the sweet odor of pot that exudes from their children's clothing when they get in the car afterwards? Don't they question why their kids have such giddy laughs and spaced-out looks when they get home? Could it be that some parents would rather not believe the truth and keep their heads in the sand?

When speaking on the subject of rock music in a personal appearance, I often illustrate my point by showing samples of record albums that are currently on the charts. The obscene and perverted pictures on the jackets are enough to give some parents cardiac arrest.

I recall one mother who vented her horror on me. "How dare you disgrace the house of God," she said, "by showing such trash. I don't need to know about those things."

Her rebuke continued in the most scathing terms until she finally walked out in a storm of disgust. The next night at the conclusion of the service, I saw her coming again. Thinking I was in for another lecture, I did my best to avoid her. Eventually she got my attention.

"I owe you an apology," she said. "When I got home last night

I went straight to my son's room to check out his record collection. To my shock, I discovered that he had nearly every album you talked about."

She went on to tell how the rest of the evening was spent with her son.

"I asked him to go through the album jackets with me and tell me something about each group. At first, he was a little reluctant. I guess he thought I only wanted to condemn him, but after a while he opened up and even showed me the lyric sheets that come with a lot of the albums. Reading what those words really say was quite a jolt to my system."

She went on with her description. "I did my best not to react self-righteously and instead put the burden back on him with questions like, 'Do you really think it's wise to fill your mind with that kind of outlook on life?' and 'Does the image that group presents really reflect the kind of values that God would be pleased with?' "

Here was a mother who, instead of merely rebuking her son's musical tastes, was really trying to understand his world without being judgmental. Of course, she had every reason to be concerned about the spiritual consequences of the music he was absorbing. But she was honest enough to admit that it was her ignorance and oversight that had allowed him to purchase those albums in the first place.

"Finally," she continued her story, "I got him to actually play some of the albums for me. I told him not to spare me and pick the wildest record he had. He chose KISS. By the time they got through describing the trigger on their 'love gun,' and telling of the girl who wants them to 'inject her,' I thought I'd literally be sick. By the look on my son's face, for once he wasn't so sure he liked the words either."

She went on to tell how they had prayer together when it was all over. They both determined that Christ would be glorified in their home.

"The turning point came," she concluded, "when I confessed to him some of my failings as a parent. He's never heard that coming from me before. I left his room knowing for the first time that I understood a little about the influences in my son's life. He didn't get rid of those records on the spot. That might have been too much to expect. What is more important is that once again I'm talking with my son. Now, the symptom will take care of itself."

Parents, it will do you no good to just condemn the music your kids listen to. At least they need to know your objections aren't based on some vague dislike for modern forms of musical expression. This book should help, and following the example of the mother I've just described will be a positive step in finding out one thing a parent can do.

TWELVE
OF COURSE
I LOVE MY CHILDREN

Most concerned parents would consider it an insult to be asked
if they really love their family. The answer to them seems
obvious. But is their love that apparent to their children?

It's true that loving is doing. We direct our time and energy
toward those objects of our affection. But don't assume
that because you house, clothe, and feed your child that he
automatically sees it as an expression of love. He's part of a welfare
state generation that tends to see the necessities of life as
rights, not privileges. What you provide for him may be too easily
seen as merely the fulfillment of a parental obligation.

My wife knows that I love her. My faithfulness, devotion, and
material provisions are proof of that. But she still likes to
be told, and more than once a day. She constantly needs that
affectionate reinforcement to feel secure in our relationship. Most
wives—and husbands—are the same. So are children.

The question should be obvious. When was the last time you
verbalized your affections to your child? You mean it, so why is it
hard for you to look your child in the eyes and simply say,
"I love you"?

Certainly, not all families are in this position. But my
experiences in counseling tell me that in the majority of homes,
verbal expressions of love and appreciation are sporadic
at best. The reason "I love you" is so hard to say is that the
utterance of those three words must be based on a foundation

of frequent and open communication. Otherwise, the words seem forced and shallow.

One evening I spoke on the subject of reconciliation in the home. I asked those who needed a healing in their families between parent and child to come forward for prayer. When they had responded, we led everyone to the prayer room and arranged for them to be seated in family units. The chairs were situated in a circle facing each other.

Before having any time of prayer or teaching, I suggested that each group spend a few moments discussing their problems. My intention was to have them begin to resolve some of their internal conflicts on their own before I offered any advice and direction.

What took place was revealing. While I waited for the ensuing conversations, there was almost total silence. Most of them just sat there staring awkwardly at each other. They were obviously very uncomfortable and not used to such direct personal confrontations with family members. In such an environment, how could parents calmly express love for their children? They couldn't even bring themselves to discuss the weather, let alone deeply felt emotions.

Before our time of counsel had been concluded, it was obvious that their conduct in that prayer room was merely a confirmation of their normal patterns at home. Lest the point be missed, let me state it succinctly. The reason your child sits in his room with the radio or stereo on full blast may be because you'd have nothing to say to him if he did come down to talk.

For three years I traveled as a professional lecturer representing a secular lyceum agency and a university. My talk was presented as an analysis of America's rock culture. Each lecture began with the following statement: "I could walk out here and ridicule your parents or curse God and most of you wouldn't do a thing. But if I said one word against your favorite rock group, some of you would tear me limb from limb."

Almost without exception that remark would be met with retorts of "You bet," or "Right on," or "You'd better believe it."

Why? Because rock is something more than just a form of music. To teens today it is a way of life that nearly consumes their every waking moment. Rock actually means more to them than their parents, because its culture has become a surrogate family. You may say "I love you" to your kids, but so do their rock stars.

In defense you might respond, "Sure, but the love in rock songs is cheap affection that's only expressed to eroticize young people or get their money. You don't suppose that my daughter really thinks that Shaun Cassidy or Mick Jagger love her?"

Probably not. But in the absence of your expressed parental affection and open communication, what may be obvious to you may not be so apparent to your child.

In times of counseling with teenagers, I've often asked them this question: "If you had deeply personal needs or problems, to whom would you go for advice?"

The list of prospects often includes friends, school counselors, clergy, or even casual acquaintances. In fact, teenagers readily discuss with me things they have never told their parents. That's tragic. Parents should not be a last resort in time of need and stress. Their counsel should be sought constantly.

Why don't parents top the list? Moms and dads should ask themselves these questions:

"Am I too busy to spend casual time with my children?"

"Am I aware of what's going on in their world?"

"Can they freely talk with me about *anything* at any time?"

"Do they know that I really love them and do I tell them so?"

If your answer is "No" to any one of these questions, you will have some clues as to why there are so few lines of communication with your child. Just stop for a moment and listen to the songs they're hearing. For money or for worse, their rock poets are saying, "We understand your problems. We care about you. Come get high with us 'cause we've got the answer. And if we can't help, go to bed with somebody who can."

That message may be false, but you've got to admit that when they absorb it all day long, it can become pretty convincing. Your child may know down inside that you love him and care about his welfare. But unless he *hears* you say what you feel for him in your heart, it won't do much good.

One final word of caution. When you express that love, let it be based on *who* your child is, not *what* he's done. Affection based on achievement is hollow. Don't wait until your kid comes home with all A's on his report card to say, "We're proud of you." God may not have blessed you with a quarterback or a cheerleader, and even though *you* know your child is the smartest one in his class, the *teacher* may not agree.

Young people can see through that kind of phony affection. They know when Mom and Dad only want them to excel because of personal pride. The rock scene accepts them just as they are, dirty jeans, C grades, adolescent frustrations, and all. When they get the message from you that acceptance is based on accomplishment, some rock singer may appeal to them as being more honest. That's why his poster is on your child's wall.

By all means, praise the successes of your children, but also understand their failures. Perhaps their expertise isn't what you planned. It's frustrating to be the child of a father who likes to hunt and fish if your interests are in art and music. Expect the best of them and teach them to strive for excellence. But don't let your pride or expectations exceed the gifts and abilities God has given them.

Love them because they're yours, God's gift of life, and you'll always be number one in their eyes. More important, they'll *really* know you care about them.

THIRTEEN
MY DAD CAN LICK YOUR DAD

Nearly every youngster is convinced that his dad is a superman
and his mother is a movie star. Part of growing up is coming
to the realization that one's mother may not be the world's most
beautiful woman and one's father not the strongest this side
of Atlas.

Yet, somehow, there's always a little bit of the child in all of us.
My dad is seventy years old, and I still think there are things
nobody can do quite as well as he can. No one can bake a pie as
good as my mom's. There are many great people I admire,
but my parents are still my heroes. And they always will be.

They aren't perfect. I've been around long enough to see all the
chinks in their armor. But God told me to honor them, and
gave me the innate capacity to do it. Their example has earned
that respect. They've seen a lot of ups and downs. I've watched
their bouts with disappointment and sickness. Nevertheless,
today their faith in God is stronger than ever.

God didn't make parents perfect. He did command them to set
an example. That example won't always be without error.
However, there is no excuse for hypocritical inconsistencies that
can be avoided by honesty and commitment to Christ.

One evening I sat in the home of a wealthy businessman in
Bogotá, Colombia, South America. Colombia is now the major
supplier of drugs to North America. The observations of
this businessman were revealing.

"Visit our jails," he said, "and you'll find no Colombian youth there, only Americans. Our children are trained from babyhood never to touch drugs. Valium is available over the counter here without a prescription. Still, good Colombian parents won't touch it. To take tranquilizers would be a hypocritical example. How, then, could we tell our children not to take drugs?"

The message for parents is simple. Your children want to follow your example. Just give them something to look up to.

Incidents of adult hypocrisy would be endless, but there's one area that teenagers frequently bring up whenever the subject of music is raised. It's the most closely associated symbol of inconsistency that bugs them when their parents knock rock. The first thing teenagers point to is the music that so many Bible-belt, middle-American adults turn on to—country and western.

Most adults are stunned when they finally learn the lyrical content of the rock tunes their children have been listening to. Why have they never noticed the words of their favorite country songs? Let the preacher knock rock and Dad will shout, "Amen!" Then, after the service, he gets in the car, tunes to the country station, and all the way home listens to songs telling of truck drivers who shack up with waitresses or go to honky tonks to drown their sorrows in booze.

Triangle affair songs and casual adultery, lubricated with liquor, provide the main subject matter. Which is worse—Rod Stewart singing "Hot Legs" or Conway Twitty declaring "You've never been this far before"? The Rolling Stones may not be paragons of moral virtue, but are they any worse than the erotically enhanced image of big-bosomed Dolly Parton, sexually precocious Tanya Tucker, or "Outlaw Blues" Waylon? The promiscuous escapades of rock entertainers may horrify Mom, but why does she buy the records of multiple divorcee Tammy Wynette? Is the sultry performance of rock singer Linda Ronstadt really any worse than country artist Barbara Mandrell singing "Married, but not to each other"?

The frankness and titillating explicitness of country songs is embarrassing. "With your blouse halfway open," sings Tommy Overstreet, "Don't go City on me." In "Cheap Perfume and Candlelight," Bobby Borchers tells his lover that if she can't make it at home, to make it any way she can. David Houston sings of the "No Tell Motel" ("We're here all night... cheatin' has become our way of life.") Johnny Duncan gets right to the point when he declares "She can put her shoes under my bed anytime."

Not to be outdone, the female artists respond with equal bluntness. Sammi Smith says, "I'll let you touch me," but adds, "It just won't feel like cheating with you." "Soft Lights and Slow Sexy Music," are recommended by Jody Miller. Jeannie Seely leaves nothing to the imagination by suggesting, "Take me to bed (and I'll be good)." Today's female country singers have punctured the God-fearing, powder-puff image of the past. With lines like "the door is always open, and the light's on in the hall," chastity is a detriment to the image of some country music-singing gals.

If there are still some diehard country fans among the parents reading this book, just check out the titles of some of the recent hits: "I Love That Woman Like the Devil Loves Sin," "It's All Wrong But It's All Right," "Out of My Head and Back in My Bed," "What Did I Promise Her Last Night," "Bedroom Eyes," "Would You Lay with Me in a Field of Stone," "Wake Up on the Warm Side of You," "I Cheated on a Good Woman's Love," "When the Fire Gets Hot," "It's a Cheating Situation," "I Just Can't Stay Married to You," "Do You Ever Fool Around," "Put Your Clothes Back On," and "Undercover Lover."

What disturbs young people the most is the veneer of religious hypocrisy that glosses over the country music scene. Such artists think nothing of singing the praises of stolen love one minute and switching to "Amazing Grace" the next. Two of the biggest country hits of recent years, "Heaven's Just a Sin Away" and "It Don't Feel Like Sinnin' to Me," were recorded by singers who claim to be staunch church members.

A well-known gospel quartet recently hit it big on the country charts with a secular song in which the lead singer brags about his sexual conquests before meeting "the one" lady of his dreams. Their follow-up song was about prostitutes in the "Ya'll Come Back Saloon." Is it any wonder your child may want you to clean up your own backyard before trampling on his?

If we dropped the subject now, enough might have been said to convince the anti-rock, pro-country music fan of his double standard. But let's not fail to mention that sex isn't the only subject in country songs. Topic number two is alcohol.

Songs praising booze include, "Red Wine and Blue Memories," "Two More Bottles of Wine," "Whiskey Trip," "The Power of Positive Drinking," "Heaven was a Drink of Wine," and "Bartender Blues." Strange, too, that parents who loudly denounce the hippie, anti-establishment ways of rock groups, in turn, cheer wildly as Johnny Paycheck sings "Take This Job and Shove It."

Remember, Mom and Dad, when you were a kid? Floyd Tillman sang of promiscuously "Slipping Around" and Hank Thompson declared "Swing Wide Your Gates of Love." You'll have to admit that things in country music haven't gotten much better. Oh, sure, there are train songs, homesick songs, and God-Bless-America songs. But they're not in the majority.

Conway Twitty, one of the foremost country stars, when reflecting on his twenty-one years as an entertainer had this to say: "As a country artist, I'm not proud of a lot of things in my field. There is no doubt in my mind that we are contributing to the moral decline in America."[1]

Enough said? Probably. It's always easier to trample on the kids' toes than on Dad's. But before we let the subject pass, permit me to share the lyrics of a song I wrote giving my own view of country music. With that, we'll let the matter drop right on your doorstep, Mom and Dad, while your children watch to see how you pick it up.

THE COUNTRY AND WESTERN SONG

Merle, Buck and Porter, Waylon, Willie, Dolly too,
Sing truck drivin', drinkin' tunes and songs to make you blue,
Honkey, tonkin' angels aren't the kind you'll meet some day,
If I may correct their song, "Hell's just a sin away."

Triangle affair songs always take the biggest part,
All the time it seems that someone's breakin' someone's heart,
If those singers really lived those songs they'd most be dead,
From exhaustion getting in and out of all those beds.

Country-western music doesn't have a sexy beat,
It's not like that rock and roll to get you on your feet,
Parents tell their kids the Rolling Stones they shouldn't hear,
But those country music words would burn a sailor's ears.

All they sing about is just unhappiness and strife,
And how someone's sleepin' with somebody else's wife,
But before they close the show and bid you all goodnight,
They toss in a hymn of faith to make it seem all right.

I'll admit that country singers don't have freaky hair,
Okies from Muskogee don't snort cocaine everywhere,
They're not like the rock stars who take dope to get along,
They're just drunk on liquor while they sing those truckin' songs.

Someday when your death has come and you have said goodbye,
Then I wonder if you'll see a jukebox in the sky,
Filled with all the country songs you've heard along the way,
To check out where you belong when it comes judgment day.

Copyright, 1978
Bob Larson
Used by Permission

FOOTNOTES

[1]*People*, Sept. 3, 1979, p. 82.

FOURTEEN
A RECORD-BREAKING EVENT

Dear Mr. Larson:

I'm writing to tell you of an important decision I just made. Last night I broke all my rock albums that I felt were hindering my Christian life. I feel so good inside. For the first time, I am really free to serve the Lord.

It wasn't easy to do. In fact, the first time I read one of your books, it made me so mad I threw it across the room. But what you said stayed with me and I started watching to see how my life was influenced by the music I heard.

You were right. I began to notice myself accepting more tolerant attitudes toward sex and God. My music was gradually brainwashing me until I almost quit serving the Lord completely.

I only wish other teenagers like me could know the joy that comes from making a full commitment to Christ. Please pray for me that I can stick by my decision.

Sincerely,
Randy

As a parent, you're probably wishing that Randy were your son. His decision is the kind that you'd like your son or daughter to make. You're concerned about the kind of music they listen to. If only they could see for themselves the damage it is doing and break their offensive albums like Randy did.

You've got to be realistic. That's probably wishful thinking. Sure, it would be good if they could come to that kind of decision spontaneously on their own. But it's not likely, and there are several reasons why.

For one thing, teenagers who indiscriminately listen to rock can find plenty of support from other Christians. When you begin to question your child's listening habits, he can readily muster help for his position from respected leaders who advocate that Christian teens should have no concern about involvement in the rock scene.

A popular Christian youth periodical reviews secular rock albums on a monthly basis. Their glowing endorsements have included records by these artists: Elton John (an admitted bisexual); Joan Baez (a proclaimed lesbian); and other artists of questionable morality I've mentioned earlier in the book (the Doobie Brothers, Linda Ronstadt, the Eagles).

"But how," you say, "could a conscientious Christian feel comfortable in supporting such singers whose lives represent the antithesis of Christian behavior?"

Most Christian parents were raised in a rather restrictive age. What may be called "legalism" or "holiness" today was merely normative Christian conduct twenty years ago. There were some things that Christians just didn't do. No questions were asked. If Mom or the pastor said "No," that was reason enough. Today Christian young people have a whole new outlook, and to understand their more lenient life style, you need to see how different their philosophies are.

For example, a recent trend in some Christian circles has been the opening of gospel discos. A secular periodical visited such dance halls and found hundreds of young people "boogieing to the discs of gospel artists."[1] One teen disco costing $350,000 features two dance floors, laser strobes, a $35,000 sound system, and a "disco dating service." Christian singles are video-taped for replay to other Christian singles who are looking for a date.

Wake up, Mom and Dad. It's a new world. The old taboos are falling fast. Formerly restricted behavior has become accepted conduct. It's not enough to merely express shock at such trends. You also need to examine the rationale behind them.

It may seem obvious to you that an entertainer who glorifies debauchery should be avoided by Christians. You're probably perplexed that the sensuous and erotic gesticulations accompanying disco dancing would be even remotely considered a form of spiritual expression. Your wildest imagination couldn't conceive that Christ is honored by flashing lights, a throbbing beat, and undulating bodies. But to some contemporary Christians, these apprehensions are irrelevant.

A new philosophy has taken over in some Christian realms. The idea is that each person is in control of his own spiritual condition, regardless of negative outside influences. Teenagers are being told that the media represents little threat to the Christian and that music is a minor factor in the larger context of life's influences.

As one Christian periodical put it, "Sometimes rock turns ugly when it shows us our own ugliness—but it should not be censored for that. Sometimes we need to see ourselves as we really are."[2]

That perspective places undue stress on the discerning faculties of human nature. It's more realistic to acknowledge that while the spirit may be willing, the flesh is weak. That's why we are told in the Bible to "come out" from the world's value system, not wallow in its warped philosophies.

Some adults may possess the character and spiritual stability to be exposed to an onslaught of satanic ideologies without succumbing to them. But a teenager in the same position is not likely to remain unscathed. They are going through a developmental stage of life in which moral values are being formed. Is it safe to assume that they will be unimpressed by the ideas and imagery of their entertainment heroes?

It may be easy for a journalist to shoot from the hip and give the teenage mind the benefit of the doubt. However, as a parent you know how frail a young person's ability to resist cultural pressure may be. You want your child protected from, not subjected to, the objectionable songs that have been outlined in this book. You'd probably feel a lot better if your son or daughter would break his or her rock albums like Randy did.

But what will they listen to then?

FOOTNOTES

[1]*Billboard*, December 18, 1976.

[2]*Campus Life*, November, 1978.

FIFTEEN
FILLING THE VACUUM

"But there's nothing else to listen to."

That kind of emotional, categoric defense is usually encountered when it's suggested to a young person that his steady diet of rock music be diminished or broken off cold turkey. It's then the average adult finally sees how genuinely addicted to rock's heartbeat a teenager can get. He's never really learned to understand any other kinds of music. Any artistic appreciation has been stunted. To take away rock is to take away an emotional security blanket that leaves some teenagers with a musical vacuum in their lives.

Most teenagers have little interest in the classics and are bored by the middle-of-the-road pop sounds . . . but they do crave music. It's been part of their upbringing, and the thought of going through life without sounds and rhythm ever present is a pretty dismal prospect to them.

In a way, that's a sad commentary on our entire culture. People are constantly massaged in an environment of sound. Nearly every home has a radio, record player, or TV on constantly. Our cars are equipped with tape decks. Stores and restaurants ply their wares with reflex-conditioning sounds, and most offices and factories program music designed to increase productivity.

Modern man feels naked without sound to soothe his day. Christian teenagers are the worst victims of this syndrome. Seldom are they ever in a position of total quietness. Is it any wonder that they have difficulty establishing a faith that will take them through life? We are told in the Bible it is only by being still that we shall truly come to know God.

There's little comfort in lamenting the tragedy of our modern life style. We're all part of it, like it or not. Though we may find occasional times of quietness to be alone and hear God speak, we have to function in the real world. Out there we are all being enveloped in the sounds of music.

Where does this conclusion lead us? If the younger generation has been programmed to develop an affinity for musical surroundings, do we fight this trend or take advantage of it? Fighting it is a practical impossibility unless you plan to pack up your family and move to the Hindu Kush. How, then, can we turn to good that which was meant for evil?

The answer is simple. Show young people that there is something else to listen to: Christian music that speaks to them in an idiom that they will find acceptable and enjoyable.

In the last decade a dramatic upheaval has taken place in contemporary Christian music. As a result, a diversity of recorded sounds is available to inspire faith, to minister to deep needs, and to simply enjoy.

Not all of these developments have been entirely positive, and there have been some rough spots along the way. In the early seventies the impact of the Jesus Revolution spawned a new generation of singers, song writers, and musicians who wanted to sing about their Savior in a way their peers could understand. Instead of solemnly warbling to the accompaniment of an organ and piano, they plugged in their guitars and set the drums beating.

Overzealousness and naiveté seemed to dominate their efforts. Anything that had the name of Jesus tacked on to it was seen as a positive influence. When George Harrison extolled Hinduism in "My Sweet Lord" and Jewish composer Norman Greenbaum unscripturally spoke of Christ as a "Spirit in the Sky," few seemed to care. What if Jesus was being portrayed as a confused and doubting revolutionary in *Jesus Christ Superstar* or an imbecilic clown in *Godspell?* At least he was a topic of discussion.

Not only were such secular rip-offs being unduly praised, but the resistance from the church to those first stirrings of new sounds was met with all too frequent belligerence. Those who

counseled caution were met with "pietized pragmatism."
"If it brings souls to Jesus," detractors were told, "then the results
justify the means."

A new day of church music was obviously dawning, but the
change came too abruptly for most Christian leaders to cope with.
Many people were concerned that a philosophy of expediency
was being too uncritically pursued. Often, such objections were
met with a hipper-than-thou attitude. "If the church won't
bend," many musicians concluded, "we'll just roll right over it."

Roll they did, rocking all the way. When adults who were
nurtured on George Beverly Shea expressed shock, they were
asked, "Why should the devil have all the good music?" Words
like "relate" and "communicate" became sacred cows.
Often, little care was taken as to the musical form with which
Christ was presented. Telling people about him was the
goal, and how it was done mattered little to some.

The sounds and jargon of the world were echoed back with a
mixture of entertainment and evangelism. "If Luther borrowed
from his culture," many asked, "why not assimilate ours
and reflect it in a Christian context?" But unlike the reformer who
extracted most of his songs on a level of excellence, these
guitar-toting minstrels tended to gravitate to the lowest
denominator of pop culture.

In spite of the apparent sincerity of these young musicians, the
early days of Jesus Music were often earmarked by attempts
to show a bubbly, groovy side of the Christian life. The lyrics were
sometimes weighted too much in favor of subjectivity and
ambiguity. An authentic, contemporary Christian form of
expression was hard to find. The trends of the world were merely
copied with little concern for originality.

Whatever other reservations may have been expressed
regarding this new musical awakening, one thing could not be
denied. The church world was feeling the reverberations
of the secular realm where virtually the entire music industry
had been taken over by those under thirty. For the first
time, the control of Christian musical expression was slipping
from the status quo hands of adult leadership.

Teenagers were no longer quietly subservient in following the
musical tastes of their elders. They now had their own
music. Its spiritual shallowness and frivolity was overlooked. At

least they were no longer bored by the unrelenting diet of anthems and hymns they felt were outdated.

As the beat of contemporary Christian music grew louder and stronger, voices of dissent were raised. Mine was one of them. I saw something disturbing taking place in the often defiant rejection of strict biblical guidelines for musical expression. A poor imitation of the world's music and life styles was not the way to reach sin-sick kids who were looking for a way out. Musically endorsing their frustrations was not the way to lift them up to Christ's level. It was catering to their immature musical tastes with a false perspective on Christian living that ignored the sacrifice of the cross.

Quite frankly, I saw no hope that an authentic, spiritually viable idiom of musical expression could come out of such confusion. It didn't seem possible that these gospel rock artists would ever mellow and mature into composers and singers who would explore themes of depth and commitment worthy of acceptance by the church. But in many ways, I was dead wrong!

I also made another, more serious miscalculation. Though I may have spoken stridently, I, too, was part of a new generation looking for new ways to make the name of Jesus known. The reservations and objections I expressed were designed to purify, not stifle; however, as a young writer I seriously under-estimated the prejudiced inertia of the evangelical church.

To my shock, my views of caution were taken much further than I had intended. The point at which I considered rock an unacceptable form of musical expression was much less restrictive than most adults interpreted it as being. In fact, some parents turned thumbs down on anything that even smacked of being "contemporary." The mere sight of guitars and drums in God's house was considered a pollution of the sanctuary.

As a critic, I tried to carefully think through my apprehensions. It was because of a genuine burden to see young people develop an honest form of musical expression that I voiced strong objections to the spiritual superficiality around me. I learned too late that many parents endorsed my cautions out of prejudice, not empathy.

Then something unfortunate happened. While I was expressing doubt and concerns about the direction of Christian music, many adults were preparing for war. The contemporary sounds of ne early seventies were declared a battleground upon which faith itself was disputed. Parents found themselves at odds with their own children who couldn't understand what all the fuss was about.

Instead of pointing out the shallow and commending the good, too many church leaders dug in their heels for a fight to the finish. That only caused some young musicians to push the boundaries even further. The conflict raged between those who wanted musical expression with no restrictions and those who were determined to venerate the past. All the while, the guitars kept right on strumming and the tunes kept right on coming.

Today, the evangelical church has entered into a whole new world. Music albums are the fastest growing aspect of the Christian bookseller industry. Many stores report that 50 percent of their dollar volume lies in Jesus Music records. Contemporary Christian music is alive and well.

The air waves are filled with it. In the United States, over 2500 stations program some gospel music. A number of stations have devoted entire formats to contemporary sounds. Top-forty gospel music charts now list the current popularity of the latest releases. What's significant about this is that not long ago, there weren't enough albums recorded to even make a chart.

Christian music is big business. Big name artists like Pat Boone, Paul Stookey, Richie Furay, B. J. Thomas, and Phil Keaggy, to mention a few, produce albums that compete commercially in the secular marketplace. One record label sells enough albums to keep twenty-three sales representatives on the road constantly.

Jesus festivals draw thousands of people to gatherings that are reminiscent of the old brush arbors. Uplift is combined with outreach to feature Bible teachers and high-energy music. Like mini-Woodstocks (minus the sex and drugs), these happenings have made Jesus cheers as common as "How Great Thou Art."

Not everyone is entirely happy to see these developments. But no one can deny that the church has entered a new era and music is leading the way. No longer can those amplified sounds be ignored by parents as an obnoxious fad. The clock is not going to go backward, so the best thing to do is understand what is happening and make plans for the future.

The vacuum is being filled. Christian young people who can be convinced to forsake the degenerate sounds of secular rock have somewhere else to turn. Their local Christian bookstore has stacks of albums by contemporary artists whose music and mode of expression reflect the thinking of young minds. The moods and feelings of adolescent longings are explored with lyrics that are often perceptive and challenging.

These may sound like strange words coming from one who initially objected to some of the trends that have brought us to this day, but I am more than happy to acknowledge the increasing quality and depth of contemporary Christian musical expression.

Parents, don't get hung up on the emotional content of words like "rock." In fact, the all-inclusive term "Jesus Music" has been adopted to reflect the wider appeal of modern Christian music. Much of what goes under the heading of "Christian rock" bears little resemblance to either the shallow offerings of the early seventies or the raucous rock of the secular world.

Just as our whole culture has calmed from the strident protests of the Vietnam days, so the youth culture of the church has also softened its attack on tradition. Their music has mellowed to accommodate a ballad style more suitable to discerning expression. Acoustic sounds mix more with the electric, and the lyrics have evolved into statements of more maturity and subtlety.

Contemporary Christian artists no longer are content to be backed by a meager gathering of mediocre musicians. It is not uncommon for an album's production to cost $15,000 to $30,000. The result is a sound in which the teenager being weaned from the world of KISS and Cooper can find enjoyment.

This is not to suggest that all current developments in the Jesus Music scene are positive and praiseworthy. However, even the worst attempts at expressing the Christian's faith in modern vogue are bound to be better than the sex-drenched paeans to hedonism found in the secular marketplace. But caution still needs to be taken lest the teenager, rebounding from the unregenerate world of rock, "jump out of the frying pan . . ."

SIXTEEN
INTO THE FIRE

But some of that Christian music doesn't sound much better than the secular rock my children are listening to now.

In some respects you may be right.

Well, then, what good will it do to encourage them to buy contemporary Christian music records?

In the first place, the words of the songs won't be saturated with references to sex and drugs. Second, the musicians are people who have given their talents to the Lord. Most of them are genuinely concerned about lifting up Jesus, not glorifying the satyric approach to life that preoccupies so much of secular rock.

Are all Jesus musicians like that? I've heard that some Christian groups are just as ego-centered as the secular ones. They seem to be as concerned about the commercial success of their music as the unsaved entertainers.

Some of them are. That's a serious problem, but don't let the antics of a few groups color your thinking about all of them.

Well, I'll concede that most of them are probably sincere. Sure, they exhibit a Christian testimony and their lyrics focus on Jesus. But the music is still the same. It's got that THUMP—THUMP beat.

A lot of the songs do. Some of the musicians lay down a beat as heavy as anything ever churned out by Led Zeppelin. But those kinds of groups are in the minority.

I'm confused. All that music sounds alike to me.

That's part of the problem. Most adults aren't tuned into the wide variety of contemporary pop sounds. It's true that teenagers often have a stunted sense of musical appreciation, but some parents also lack an awareness of the diversity found in both secular and Christian contemporary music. Just as their children tend to categorize Mom's music as "slow and boring," Mom also tends toward an overly critical and categoric view of harmonies and rhythms that are unfamiliar.

The whole field of Jesus Music is young and growing. It's got a lot of shortcomings and sometimes these inconsistencies are the easiest to see. Remember, most of these musicians are filled with the zeal and idealism of youth. They want to get the job done as quickly as possible. Often their impetuousness gets the best of them and the short-range goal overpowers larger and wider concerns. Maturity has a way of mellowing the most fervent zealot. But most young musicians haven't had the chance yet to view their art from the perspective of history.

I agree with all that. But the beat still bothers me.

Your concern is legitimate and deserves a response. But you also need to be cautious. Approaching the subject will require total honesty from you as a parent.

There's just no way to take the subject of Christian music and define its scope and limitations in a way that will satisfy everyone. We're all unique beings with divergent backgrounds of culture and tastes. That's what makes life so exciting. Your likes and dislikes are in part a product of God's special way of forming your life. If we all liked only chocolate cake and loved the same woman (or man), it would be a very dull world. Sameness is stifling while diversity is enriching.

Keep in mind that because music is a form of individual and cultural expression, there is no way to achieve unanimity for the entire body of Christ. One Sunday morning in India, I preached for a group of Tamil Indian Christians. Their song service was a shock to my system. The banging of drums mingling with a variety of cymbals and untuned guitars sounded like pure cacophony to me. But the smiles on their faces radiated a love for Christ that transcended our dissimilar upbringings.

Do you enjoy anthems, solemnity, and pipe organ preludes? Is

that your estimation of what epitomizes a true atmosphere
of worship and adoration? That's fine, but don't try to impose your
evaluation on a black congregation in the Caribbean Islands.
I've watched them sing and sway with an enthusiasm that would
bring an infectious smile to the face of all but the most somber
deacon.

God can't be put in a box. Try it, and he breaks out to fill and
inspire those parts of his body that are willing to respond
spontaneously to the Spirit. Creativity is a gift from God, and what
man is to say how the Lord will channel that gift? Believe
me, I've tried in many areas of life to fence God in, and it didn't
work. And nearly every preacher who has said God *wouldn't*
or *couldn't* has later had to eat his words or retrench into an
ecclesiastical, legalistic fortress.

Am I suggesting that anything goes? Never. But I am counseling
a discerning and compassionate approach to this volatile
subject of what perimeters apply to Christian music. There are no
neatly structured boxes that give absolute guidelines in this area.

As a parent, it would be easier for you if there were a
formula to go by. Any Christian music that was applicable would
be permissible for your children to listen to. That which
would be outside of this endorsement would be taboo.
Unfortunately, this kind of idealistic categorization just isn't
realistic.

*What is a parent to do? I'll try to be honest and not condemn
all contemporary Christian music. But aren't there some
restrictions that my children should adhere to? Where do I draw
the line?*

Perhaps before we go any further it would be wise to pause for a
moment and think about the Source of music. Why does
music exist? What is its purpose for mankind and the church?

Satan may lay claim to using music for the widest extent
of expression and effect, but he didn't write the first song. Music
sprang from the heart of God who gave this gift to man for his
pleasure and enrichment. When we see the handiwork of God and
experience his love in our own lives, we have no right to
be silent. God fashioned our lips and lungs to sing forth praises and
thanksgiving to him. Our hands have been endowed with the
ability to construct instruments upon which we may make melody
to harmonize with the song of Creation.

Again and again, the Bible records those times when God's people burst forth with music and singing to honor the exploits of the Lord. When the Israelites crossed the Red Sea, they sang of their deliverance. In the Psalms, David set to music the joys and anguish of his heart. It was he who arranged for thousands of musicians to accompany the Ark of the Lord. The sound of it all must have been magnificent as the singers blended with psalteries, trumpets, harps, and cymbals. David's song of 1 Chronicles 16 exemplifies how music can be a declaration of faith as well as joy.

When Jesus came into the world, his annunciation was not heralded by a written decree worthy of a king. Once again God chose the medium of music to reach man's heart. The great event was made known by a chorus of angels who serenaded simple shepherds. The nocturnal declaration fulfilled the prophecy of the Magnificat sung by the Virgin to magnify the Lord.

The New Testament records that singing filled the hearts of believers who had found their Messiah. God shook a prison when Paul and Silas sang. Ephesians 5:19 and Colossians 3:16 make it obvious that music was soon incorporated into worship gatherings. "Is any merry?" the Apostle James asked, "let him sing psalms."

One of the most glorious anticipations of the church is to join the saints of the ages in a great songfest. The psalmist spoke in Psalms 40:3 and 98:1 of a "new song" that he longed for to consummate his faith. In our age that song is ready to spring forth at any moment.

As Jehoshaphat sent forth musicians to precede and proclaim the victory of the Lord, he stood still to see God's salvation. It is only fitting that Christians who now await that final triumph should be bursting forth with song. Our salvation, too, is soon to be revealed when we shall gather around the throne of God. Our "new song" in that day, described in Revelation 5:9, will be an unending anthem of praise to our Savior.

But the "new song" of the Lord is not yet a clarion melody to either the world or the church. Satan too often infiltrates its purity with his old song. It is the devil's music that we need to abhor with an intensity equal to our appreciation of the Lord's song.

While it is clear that God is the Source of music, it is also apparent from Ezekiel 28:13 that Satan was the first musician. But his song which once resounded about God's throne turned into a dirge of death when he rebelled against the Almighty. Since that day the devil has had the world dancing to his tune.

Like every good gift of God, music has often been perverted to serve Satan's ends. He who once played on the tabrets and pipes the song of the Lord, afterwards skillfully constructed sounds that would facilitate the worship of those evil angels who fell with him. Even God's own people gave heed unto the "chant to the sound of the viol" until he declared, "Take away from me the noise of your songs" (Amos 5:23; 6:5).

But though entire nations could be deceived into bowing before Satan's sounds, God always found men whose ears were tuned to the Lord's melody. Shadrach, Meshach, and Abednego refused to heed the tune of the cornet, flute, harp, sackbut, psaltery, and dulcimer. They were not offended by the tones, harmonies, and rhythms of these instruments. On the contrary, the Lord himself had sanctioned the sound of these musical inventions elsewhere in his Word. It was not the music but the *motive* that mattered.

Their refusal was not based on the virtuosity, talent, performance, or melodic construction of the music. A fiery furnace was hardly worth enduring for a mere difference over musical tastes. What they did count a sufficient reason for not heeding the musical supplication was the pagan purpose behind it all. This is a valuable lesson we need to observe.

It is not the technical aspects of a musical composition that render its intent good or evil, but how it is played and why it is played does matter greatly. When music is truly directed toward the glorification of God, it becomes a valuable asset to inspiring faith. But when a song only lifts up the singer, such egocentricity has no place in Christian worship or evangelism.

I have had the privilege of traveling to more than seventy countries around the world. As a student of religions, I have been able to make many valuable observations regarding the impact that belief systems can have on a culture. One of the more obvious conclusions I have drawn is that no religion outside of Christianity has so generously incorporated music as a means of expression. Even the heathen and agnostic must admit that the greatest music of human history owes a debt of inspiration to the Christian faith.

I have walked among Hindus, Taoists, Buddhists, Moslems, and other devotees of major religions. While music does play a minor role in worship and devotion, there is nothing to compare with the centrality of music to Christianity. The reason seems apparent. Faith in Christ alone is devoid of appeasement and ritualism. Our love for our Savior ushers forth with a spontaneity and exuberance that is founded on love. The heart of a true believer cannot help but sing.

So much for why we sing and from whom our song comes. But what kind of song should we sing? Does the character and quality of Christian music play a role in determining its effect?

It seems axiomatic to state that music about God should be like God. His beauty, love, harmony, consistency, mercy, peace, and graciousness should be part of our songs. Not every tune needs to embody all the attributes of God. There is room for the subjective expression of one's personal view of faith as well as the more colloquial statements of the folk idiom. However, one rule is unavoidable—the lyrics should never depart from scriptural presuppositions that direct the hearer to thoughts about God's works and ways.

But what of the music itself? Are there any guidelines or restrictions by which the appropriateness of the musical structure is evaluated? Obviously, lyrics are the first priority for consideration. Provided that the content is consistent with the principles we've already considered, does the melody and rhythm need to be as closely scrutinized for deficiencies? Let's return to our axiom: music about God should be like God. How does that apply to a Jesus Music group with amplified instruments and a decibel capability to blast out a rhythmically pulsating sound?

On a very practical level, it seems that the less pure the motive, the louder and wilder the music. A group that plays to lift up Jesus will not concentrate on the mere execution of showmanship to entertain an audience. There are exceptions to this rule, but the heavier the group's sound, the more commercial their intent may be.

This is not to suggest that a mellow acoustic arrangement is necessarily sanctified. There are times when God speaks

with bite and punch to his words. One can only wonder what
would happen in some decorous church gatherings if someone
were to take seriously the psalmist's suggestion to, "Praise him
upon the loud cymbals." Such a foolhardy person would
probably be ejected immediately from the sedate setting.

Some evangelicals have a real hang-up regarding drums.
Immediately after my conversion from the world of rock music, I
did too. It wasn't long before the Lord shattered my prejudice.
While visiting New Zealand I was privileged to hear a drum
solo performed by a newly saved jazz musician. To the accompaniment of a Scripture reading, he audibly demonstrated the
attributes of God.

When God thundered from heaven, his bass drum nearly burst.
The cadence of his snare brought forth visions of the marching
armies of the hosts of the Lord. As God descended on Sinai
in power and majesty, he launched into a flurry of rolls and cymbal
crashes. At the conclusion I was breathless. What many
would consider "the devil's instrument" had ushered me into the
presence of God and destroyed my bias in the process.

Can drums ever get out of hand in a song? Yes, if they are used
to drive a song to the point of eliciting sensual impulses.
A drummer who is a sensitive musician led by the Holy Spirit can
inspire one's emotions by heightening physical responses.
But an undiscerning drummer can use his sticks to eroticize an
audience and create unhealthy urges that conflict with any
Christian purpose in a song.

Christian music should be primarily designed to touch the head
and the heart. When it only appeals to the hip and the heel,
the spiritual benefit is diminished. The rhythm of a song should
carry, not constrict, the words. The tune that makes you
feel more like dancing than worshiping may hinder the intent of its
message. Music about Jesus should honor the gentleness of the
Holy Spirit, not insistently enforce itself upon you by the power of
its beat.

The only problem with such cautions is that they tend to be
heard through the filter of each person's prejudices. Some
musicians will see them as too restrictive while many adults will
apply them with a conservative vengeance. That's a risk that
must be taken. The only other choice is to leave the impression
that "music is music and whatever moves you must be good."

Perhaps the difference in interpretation of these cautions lies not so much in the musical divisions of the generation gap as it does in the lack of true spiritual discernment among all Christians. Man is a trichotomous being—body, soul (mind-consciousness), and spirit. Many times what is presumed to apply to the latter actually appeals to the former. Young people at some Christian concerts will boogie and bounce with abandon to the beat. As they leave, you can hear them say, "Couldn't you feel the spirit?"

Even though they are probably better off there than at the local disco, it is a sad fact of modern church life that a musically induced, physical "high" is often portrayed as a spiritual experience. "Getting off" on the music is not necessarily communicating with God. That which arouses the body and soul may not contribute to the edification of the spirit. It's not wrong when music makes one feel good. Carnality is not inherent when the body responds to a catchy rhythm. But it is erroneous and deceptive to always equate either of these effects with a Spirit-enriching encounter.

One more note of caution is worth mentioning. All music, whether evil or edifying, has the capacity to induce a spirit-transcending experience. The occult and black arts, along with various false religions, recognize this principle. That is why they use certain musical forms to create trance states or evoke an atmosphere which facilitates the operation of demon spirits.

I have personally witnessed a number of pagan self-mutilation and torture rituals in which rhythms were used to create a spiritual environment facilitating demonic control. In addition, I have also watched those involved in witchcraft practices utilize melodies and beats to help achieve an altered state of consciousness. If music can be constructed to place one on a different "spirit-level" in Satan's realm, then what does this mean to a Christian musician?

Even after one's motive and sincerity have been proven beyond question, attention must still be given to the possibility of inherent responses from the medium itself. As a master musician, Satan knows well what kinds of music tend to evoke transcendent spiritual states. Avoidance of such a potentiality should concern every artist of contemporary Christian music.

Where does this leave you when you walk in your Christian bookstore to buy a contemporary record album? First of all, you should be excited to see such a wide variety of selections available. Second, you should buy an album that will contribute spiritually through its music and message. Don't make the mistake of buying a Christian record on the same basis as you would purchase a secular album: the appeal of its sound. Certainly the quality of the arrangements will be a deciding factor. But if the commercial viability of a record's sound is your whole purpose in buying it, you have only jumped out of the frying pan into the fire.

SEVENTEEN
THANKS, MOM AND DAD

So far, this has been a book about children, for parents. It has
also been a look at communication problems in the home.
The responsibility of parents to express love and set an example
has been seen as one way to solve the dilemma. But teenagers
also have a role to play.

It's assumed that once parents have finished this book, they'll
pass it on to their children. That's why this chapter is aimed
at them with one question in mind: "When was the last time you
said, 'Thanks,' to Mom and Dad?"

Your generation is the most affluent in history. What were once
luxuries are now taken for granted. The Welfare State philosophy
has indocrinated most people with the idea that the necessities
of life are a right to be expected. Food and shelter are the
bare minimum. While former generations were content to survive
with few pleasures, people now worry about "the quality of life."

As a result, the average young person has become accustomed
to an easy access of life's provisions. The roof over their heads,
the food in their stomachs, and the clothes on their backs
are seldom given a second thought. The toil their parents endure
to make life so "easy" is almost never acknowledged. Why
should frequent expressions of thankfulness be necessary? After
all, isn't that what parents are for?

Do you know how much your parents love you? More than
anything in the world! Some parents may be self-centered

exceptions, but I haven't met many of them. Most of the moms and dads I've talked with would literally die for their children.

They brought you into this world with pain and self-sacrifice. You don't remember those dirty diapers, sleepless hours from midnight wails, and bouts with childhood diseases. But they do. Your parents know the labor of love it has taken to raise you from babyhood through childhood to adolescence. And they wouldn't trade a moment of it.

Mom and Dad watched you spill food as you insisted on using your own spoon. They gingerly launched you on your first steps and soothed the hurt when you stumbled. Then they saw you pass puberty and emerge with feelings of your own sexual identity. The love you returned to them along the way made all the heartaches and self-denial seem worth it.

When you became a teenager, something happened. Until then, you were totally dependent upon your parents. As an adolescent, you wanted to make decisions on your own. In a way that is good; it shows you had matured to the point of developing your own values system. Mom and Dad had to learn which apron strings to cut and which they needed to keep.

As a teenager, you have become your own person; not quite equal to your parents, but a separate personality with emotions and feelings that come from within. Before this, expressions of love to your mom and dad came naturally. Thanking them for special things was easy. You were totally dependent upon them and you knew it.

Now things are different. The values and restrictions of your elders often come into conflict with yours. As a child you were expected to obey without question. Today, you want answers and reasons. "No" is not enough. You also want to know "Why?"

God beautifully planned this stage of your life. He knows that someday you will have to speak up for your own convictions. Mom and Dad won't be around to protect and shelter you. It's good that you want to establish your own identity. But be careful. In the meantime, you may forget how dependent upon your parents you still are, and you may also overlook how much they still need to know that you need them.

All this boils down to one simple question: When was the last time you expressed gratitude to your parents?

Have you said "thanks" to them lately for providing the basics

of life as well as the pleasures of the extra things they do?
Why not go to them right now and say something like this:

*Dad, I know you work hard to make a living for our family. You
put in some long hours so that we can have a place to live
and food to eat. Sometimes I've taken these things for granted.
But I want you to know I do appreciate all you do for us. Thanks,
Dad.*

*Mom, you always make sure there's a meal on the table. You
even try to make a special treat when you can. While I'm
at school, you're busy making sure our house is a home. We'd sure
be in a mess without you. Thanks, Mom.*

There are obvious exceptions to this specific formula. Perhaps
your parents are separated or one of them has died. Maybe
you live in a foster home or have adoptive parents. Whatever your
particular situation, there is most likely someone God has
placed in the position of parental authority in your life. It is to
him or her you owe a sincere debt of gratitude.

If those words of thanks are hard to come by, it may be a
symptom that you have difficulty at any time when conversing
with your parents. Have you ever stopped to think about how little
time you may be spending with them? I've met many teenagers
who are better acquainted with friends, teachers, and schoolmates
than they are with their own parents. The reason is obvious.
You get to know people you talk to.

Tragically, most families only congregate to eat or watch TV.
Mealtime can hardly be considered an effective open forum
since in many homes it's a hurry-up time. Neither can viewing
television be described as an activity in which people really
get to know each other.

What about this suggestion? Spend next weekend with Mom
and Dad. Just them! Cancel your parties and plans. Leave the TV
and stereo off and get reacquainted with the two people
who love you most. When you really get to know them, you'll find
a lot to be thankful for.

EIGHTEEN
MANSION OVER THE HILLTOP

Before you hand this book back to your parents, I want to share
with you some personal experiences. The Lord has taught
me some lessons that may save you and your parents a lot of
heartache if you'll read these final two chapters carefully.

There are two things God requires of you as a child—honor and
obedience. In the Old Testament, you are told in Exodus
20:12, "Honor thy father and thy mother that thy days may be
long upon the land."

In the New Testament we read this injunction (Eph. 6:1 and
Col. 3:20): "Obey your parents."

Teenager, God promises to bless your life if you do those two
things. If you do not, the consequences are stark. In fact,
the Apostle Paul declares that the end times before the return of
Christ will be evidenced by a generation that is "disobedient
to parents" (2 Tim. 3:2).

The opposite of obedience is rebellion. That kind of conduct,
God declares, is tantamount to practicing witchcraft (1 Sam.
15:23). He also declares that stubbornness is equatable with
idolatry.

Those are pretty stern warnings, especially for this generation
for whom it has become fashionable to defy tradition and
anything considered to be of the Establishment. Many parents
are no longer able to control their children. More than
one sobbing mother has told me she can't discipline her son for
fear of physical retaliation.

"But I wouldn't do that," you argue. "I'd never strike back at my parents."

Perhaps not in a literal, physical sense. But what about the verbal and emotional abuses you may have heaped upon them? The slammed door, the pouting lip, the yelled retort are just as effective and serious.

"You're not going to run my life," you screamed, running up the stairs to your bedroom.

Then you put on the earphones and plugged into your favorite rock album. The words and sounds carried you away. The message placated your injured pride. Over and over the songs declared, "Get high. Forget the hassles. Parents don't understand. Move with the music. We're taking over someday. Kick out the jams!"

You think I'm exaggerating? Then make your own list of how many popular rock artists include their parents as part of their careers. Name the songs you've heard telling you that your parents know best and that success in life will depend upon how well you follow their advice. It's a pretty short list, isn't it?

The crazed world of sex and drugs that rock entertainers live in doesn't lend itself to reflections on parental respect. In fact, few of the superstars ever bother to mention their moms and dads. That's probably to be expected. There aren't many parents who'd be willing to publicly endorse the outlandish life styles their children have adopted.

Let's face it. The rock scene and the world at large aren't going to give you much incentive to obey and honor your parents. The only real encouragement you'll get is from God and his Word.

There are two facts about parents that most kids don't understand:

FACT #1: *Parents aren't perfect*.

"Big deal," you say. "I already knew that."

Well then, why do you act as if you expected perfection from them? Parents *do* make mistakes, and their judgment *is* fallible; but even then, in most cases, it's bound to be better than yours.

Your parents have something you can never exceed—experience. When they advise or reprimand you, it's because your best interests are foremost in their minds. When most parents do err, it's a mistake of the head, not the heart. They truly want what's best for you, and sometimes their perspective is difficult for you to understand.

You can probably name a dozen times when your parents made a wrong decision that affected your life. Before you trumpet that criticism, ask yourself how many times you'd have goofed if you would have ignored their advice and done things your way.

Nowhere does God command you to honor and obey your parents with qualifications. He doesn't demand your allegiance to them because they're perceptive, intelligent, well educated, knowledgeable, and perfect. God only requires that you obey.

If your parents make wrong decisions governing your life, God will hold them accountable, not you. On the other hand, if you disobey even their erroneous directives, you are the one he will hold accountable. (Keep in mind we are discussing Christian homes where parents are presumably trying to raise their children in the fear of the Lord. The only instance where disobedience might be justified would be in the case of a sinful parent advocating that the child indulge in unlawful or immoral behavior. In that case, obedience must be accorded to the higher law of God.)

FACT #2: *Parents don't always have a reason for the advice they give.*

"Just give me one good reason why I can't," you protest.

That plea is usually followed by the proverbial, "Everybody's doing it."

It's presumed that the wisdom of your parents is suspect in view of what you feel are overwhelming odds in your favor.

First of all, are you really so certain that "everybody" is doing it? Mary, Jack, Jane, and three other classmates do not warrant the unqualified, inclusive pronoun, "everybody." Such logic is intended to intimidate parents into submission. After all, they wouldn't want their son or daughter to be left out. It's assumed that "everybody" else's parents have given approval, so why should yours be different?

It takes a brave mom and dad to stand up to that one. But they need even more courage and fortitude to withstand the wearing-down process of, "Give me one good reason."

It's not that you really want to know why they say no. You just want them on the defensive. Instead of obediently submitting, you've placed your parents in the position of having to justify their decision.

You've already made up your mind that they're wrong. It's just

a matter of time until you can prove it. You assume they
have no right to forbid your conduct unless they can present a
rational explanation of their refusal. Is your reasoning correct?

Because God has made your parents responsible for your
behavior, he provides them with special insight to guide your life.
As a result, they may sometimes express intuitive apprehensions
for which they have no discernible logic.

God places something in the heart of a parent that can't be
explained. They may perceive inherent dangers in a course of
action you want to pursue. Sometimes they will not be able
to articulate why they feel that pitfalls are in your path. They just
feel it, and that's why they say "No."

The choice is yours. You can obey their decision and honor
them, even if it means denying something you really want. The
alternative is to ignore their denial for the sake of fulfilling
your own desires. Rejecting their advice may cause you to miss
God's richest blessings on your life.

Perhaps the following personal illustration will allow me to
convey the importance of obeying parental authority.

For several years my wife and I had wanted to move from
suburbia and relocate in a more rural, mountainous setting near
our home in Denver, Colorado. We love the outdoors and
have always felt cramped by the noise and bustle of city life.

After an extensive search, we came upon a home that
seemed just perfect for our needs. Located on a wooded acreage
not far from town, it was near enough to be convenient
and far enough away to be secluded. More importantly, it would
provide the peace and quiet we longed for when we needed
to get away from our hectic life style.

Everything was suitable but the price. There seemed to be no
way we could afford to buy the house. However, it had
been on the market for quite a while, and the real estate agent
suggested that I at least make an offer. The amount I chose
was so low he was hesitant to write up a contract for fear my offer
would be considered unreasonable.

I was even more shocked than he was when the sellers
accepted. It was too good to be true. One financial advisor assured
me that the house was underpriced, and that I could easily
double my money in a year by appreciation alone. I explained the
purchase to my accountant. Without exception, everyone I

talked with encouraged me to go through with the deal. They all felt I had come upon a once-in-a-lifetime opportunity.

Then I called my parents.

We were so excited I couldn't wait to tell them. After some preliminary small talk, I got to the point.

"Mom and Dad, remember that beautiful home in the mountains we showed you? Well, I made them a ridiculously low offer, and they accepted. We signed the contract today. Isn't that great?"

There was silence at the other end.

Their hesitation puzzled me. I couldn't imagine their having any apprehensions. Everyone else wanted us to buy it. Surely, they would agree.

Dad was the first to speak. "Don't do it, Son," he said.

I went limp. I hadn't called for their advice or consent. My mind was already made up. As a grown man, married, in my thirties, I was certainly capable of making my own decisions in life. I wasn't asking for their opinion. But now that I had it, what was I going to do?

Naturally, I did what any son would do. "Just give me one good reason," I protested.

They offered one, but it was only a feeble excuse by my estimation. I shot it full of holes with my "superior" logic.

"Give me another reason," I chided them.

This went on for several minutes. Mom and Dad would try to explain why they felt as they did. In turn, I would explode their arguments by asserting the reasonableness of our decision.

Finally, I thought they were out of ammunition, and I moved in for the kill.

"Just give me one more good reason," I insisted.

"We feel this way because we've prayed about it," they answered.

There was no retort for that one!

It did propose a nagging question to my mind. Was it possible that even at my age God could speak to me through my parents? Even though I had established my own household, did this mean I was completely beyond their jurisdiction? All this was too much for me to weigh in a moment's time.

"Kathy and I will have to talk this over and call you back later," I said.

The next twenty-four hours were agonizing. I was torn between the logic and desires of my own feelings and an impulse to obey my parents in spite of what I felt were irrational conclusions on their part.

Finally, I reached a decision.

There seemed to be no logical reason to follow my parents' advice. Their only real objection had come from a subjective, spiritual impression. I honestly felt we could buy that house without dishonoring them or disobeying the Lord.

"But perhaps God wants to take that house away from us so later on he can give us something better," Kathy reasoned.

I agreed. Another, more convincing thought came to mind.

What if we disobeyed my parents in these closing years of their lives? Could we stand by their graves knowing that when they needed us most we rejected their advice?

I called up the real estate man with whom I had signed the contract. When I informed him that we wanted to terminate the deal, he was understandably upset. Then I explained my reason why.

He listened intently and responded. "I'm Jewish," he said, "and I've always been taught to honor my parents in the same way. I won't hold you to the contract."

When he tore it up, I felt an unexplainable sense of peace. To the natural mind, my decision made no sense. But that didn't matter to us. We had obeyed my parents, and the loss of our "dream house" was a small price to pay for honoring them.

Were my parents right? It took us three years to find out that God *did* have something better for us.

NINETEEN
SHAMEA

"That house could have been yours."

I heard the devil say it a thousand times. He just wouldn't let me forget. Everytime we had to drive into the mountains on business or pleasure, he always made sure I noticed what could have been mine.

What happened to the home? It would have been easier to discover later that the foundation was eaten by termites. If it had burned to the ground, my sympathy might have exceeded my jealousy for the new owners. In fact, I resented them a little. When they immediately plunged into a remodeling job, I was amazed they could conceive of any improvements on my dream home.

I was content that our decision had been in the Lord's will, but emotionally I wanted some kind of definite confirmation that we had really done the honorable thing. I needed to *know* what I knew was right. It seems that we Christians don't mind obeying the Lord as long as we receive adequate commendation for our moral courage. Furthermore, we don't want to wait long to get it.

As the months passed on, we grew continually more dissatisfied with our typical suburban home. But we resigned ourselves to the possibility that we might have to live there for life with barking dogs, blaring stereos, hollering kids, and all. Opportunity had knocked, and we had closed the door. It seemed unlikely to call again.

The most effective antidote to the devil's taunt was Kathy's perspective: "God is taking this away from us so he can give us something better."

It's easy for God's children to forget he loves us and really wants to give us the desires of our hearts when we delight ourselves in him. Too often we see God as a stern judge who only wants to deprive and discipline us. We get the idea that self-denial and sacrifice are the only roads to happiness and forget that once we have given, he wants to give back to us in even greater measure. Instead of approaching his blessings with joy, we timidly acknowledge them with guilt.

Would you enjoy giving gifts to your children if they received them with reluctance? Christmas would be a sad time if all you heard around the tree were the words, "I really don't deserve such expressions of love." We give because we want to delight the recipient. God does too.

So many young people look at the Lord as if he only wanted to rob their adolescent years of all joy and excitement. Getting rid of that KISS album and taking down that Fleetwood Mac poster is seen as a "don't." If only they could see this kind of commitment as a "do" to open God's window of blessings.

But before God can really bless you, two things are necessary. You have to say "No" to those things which can come between you and the Lord. Second, you must be tested to determine whether you are capable of handling God's abundance. In short, you will need to prove the principle that faithfulness over a few things will make you worthy of being "ruler" over many things.

In my own life, obedience had taught me the first lesson. By honoring my parents, I had shown that my material desires came second to my concern for doing what was right. That important second test of proving my worthiness for God's blessings still lay ahead.

The Lord had for several years been leading Kathy and me into an intensive personal ministry of counseling those who were bound by evil forces. That exotic and eyebrow-raising term "demon-possession" had become as real and familiar as any other experience in God's Word. The instances of dealing directly with demons had become as common as praying with people who had less spectacular problems.

At times, we even opened our home to help such people. For them, a brief time of advice and counsel was not enough. You can't make appointments with Satan or the Holy Spirit. Freedom from spiritual enslavement often involves a prolonged struggle which requires rebuking the devil and extending trust and love to the one he has invaded. Our home had become a haven for those Satan had enslaved. It was not our "dream home" in the mountains, but for many, it was a spiritual oasis where they could drink freely of God's liberating power.

On one such occasion, we were praying with an individual who had for many years been involved in the world of spiritualism and the black arts. Through a series of miraculous circumstances, God's grace had sovereignly reached down to pluck this one from the grip of Satan.

Months of battling the devil's kingdom had reached a climax, and we were directly confronting one of the most violent and powerful spirits controlling this person. As we were seated in the family room of our home, the demon was manifesting itself through the voice, eyes, and other neurosensory apparatus of the one for whom we were interceding.

Suddenly, as I proceeded to rebuke the spirit in the name of the Lord, the person's head turned as the demon, looking out, began to stare at a shelf on our wall.

"What are you doing?" I demanded to know.

"I am drawing strength out of that object," the voice hellishly answered.

I turned quickly to see what the spirit had so intently set its eyes upon. There, in a corner of the room, was a wooden ebony carving we had purchased six years earlier on the island of Bali.

"Is that the only thing in our home that you draw power from?" I insisted on finding out.

"No," the voice answered defiantly.

For a moment, I was stunned. We had dedicated our home to the Lord, and assumed that everything we owned belonged to him. How could sin have so effectively entered into our midst?

Perhaps I should explain something about our home. It's like a museum. Our travels have provided an opportunity to collect souvenirs of our visits to nearly every part of the world. Many of these items are artifacts purchased for little in their land of origin, but worth much more over here. Other objects are mere souvenirs or presents from missionaries and grateful friends to whom we have ministered.

Among the scores of mementos that we treasure were eleven objects that contained symbolic and intrinsic expressions of Satan's kingdom. How we found them and what we did with them was God's way of testing us before pouring out the blessings he had in store.

When the demon revealed that certain possessions were hindering our spiritual effectiveness, I immediately bound the spirit by the Word of authority. Gradually, it submerged and the person came out of a trance. "Have you noticed anything in our home that affects you adversely?" I asked.

"Oh, yes," came the reply. "I've never looked to see where the vibrations were coming from, but I felt them the moment I walked in your front door."

"Well, then," I instructed, "the three of us are going to walk through every room of this house while you point out everything that might be displeasing to God."

How would you have responded to such a request? Imagine a couple graciously inviting you into their home to offer prayer and spiritual help. Then, you find yourself in the position of telling them that certain of their possessions have demonic significance. In a way, it's like biting the hand that feeds you.

We were asking a lot of this person whose hesitancy was understandable. Nevertheless, we went from room to room gathering our collection of demonically influenced artifacts.

I was astonished to find things in our home that had been overlooked for years. All of our gifts and purchases had been carefully selected. None of them was an idol or a fetish. I had always asked if there was any religious significance to the items we chose. But my caution, though commendable, had not been thorough enough.

We were shocked to find that a magnificent water color painting from Indonesia had the face of a spirit cleverly depicted in an obscure corner. An African oil of a tribal chieftain was discovered, upon closer inspection, to portray a meditative trance state. One by one, the objects were taken from walls and shelves and placed in our box of infamy.

We walked down the stairs into the basement. I knew that this

person had never before been inside my office located
there. As we stepped through the door, I asked, "Is there anything
in here that causes the spirits inside you to react?"

The reply came without a glance in any direction, "Over there,
on the left."

I looked in vain to see anything that could be a source of
satanic expression.

"It's small, about six inches high, whatever it is."

"But all I can see is a little bronze figurine of a Thai dancer I
picked up in the Bangkok airport ten years ago. It's just a
cheap souvenir," I argued.

"Look closer, at the face."

I was stunned. The face was no larger than my thumbnail. Yet
some craftsman had ingeniously etched the hideous face of a
spirit that seemed obviously out of place with the gracefully
shaped body attached to it.

Into the box it went. When the last room had finally been
surveyed, we had gathered over $3,000 worth of objects. Added to
this was an exquisitely carved wooden desk valued at $4,000.
Part of it was salvageable since only the carvings on the trim were
objectionable, but the other eleven objects left me with only
one choice.

We went back to the family room and started a fire in the
fireplace. One by one the objects were thrown into the flames, for
purification and destruction. The intensity of the heat was
amplified by the 90° weather of a hot summer's day. The room
seemed momentarily transformed into hell itself. Somehow,
the brilliant flames and searing heat seemed appropriate.

As we watched each artifact go up in smoke, a greater sense of
peace entered into our home. All the while, strange things
were happening. At one point, a scream burst out of the fire. If
Kathy had not confirmed to me that she, too, heard it, I
might have wondered for a moment if the drama of the incident
was overpowering my rationality.

Before I struck the first match, I had tried to anticipate what
my feelings would be. Would some great surge of spiritual
pride overwhelm me because of the enormity of my commitment?
After all, how many people would be willing to destroy
$3,000 worth of valued treasures?

In spite of my costly decision, all I felt was shame. Oh, to be sure, I had innocently purchased those items. If I had ever dreamed they would be a source of inspiration to Satan, I'd never have brought them into my home. Such thinking could not excuse me now.

One thought predominated in my mind: "How many times had the Holy Spirit tried to speak to me and warn me that some of my possessions were a hindrance to those I was trying to help?"

A profound sense of unworthiness filled me. It had taken an evil spirit to bring me to the place of seeing the spiritual obstacles in my life, when I should have been listening to the Holy Spirit.

It's even more tragic to realize that our situation is not unique among Christian homes. Perhaps these specific circumstances were extraordinary, but the problem is all too common. I've visited in scores of homes that have trinkets and symbols of pagan representations displayed: Aztec sun signs, Buddhas, astrology plaques, tiki gods, African devil masks, Kachina witch doctor dolls, ankh rings and pendants, and an assortment of occult and idolatrous artifacts. More people are traveling overseas, and they often return with an array of mementos that symbolize Satan's kingdom, not Christ's lordship. Some who declare that Jesus is the head of their home openly exhibit things which convey Satan's seal of ownership.

Does that mean Christians should go on a witch hunt through their homes? Should they go looking for demons under every bed? Is each strange or foreign object a source of invested satanic energy? Absolutely not! It would only glorify Satan to adopt a paranoid outlook that suspects evil in every corner.

The Christian who walks in fellowship with Christ and abides under the blood should have no fear of Satan or his devices. But neither are we to be ignorant of them. Deuteronomy 7:26 warns us, "Neither shalt thou bring an abomination into thine house lest thou be a cursed thing like it; but thou shalt utterly detest it and thou shalt utterly abhor it; for it is a cursed thing."

Don't be so foolish as to imagine that any object by itself alone can bring evil into your home. It is, ultimately, the attitude of the heart that gives place to Satan. But if one's life is spiritually vulnerable, it is a dangerous thing to harbor that which is cursed. Furthermore, the injunction of Deuteronomy 7:26 applies to more than the souvenirs of Mom and Dad. It can also encompass the record albums of the rock generation.

The next Sunday after those objects were burned in our fireplace, I preached a sermon on full surrender to Christ. Immediately after my message, a tall teenage boy walked up to me.

"Mr. Larson," he said, "I think Led Zeppelin is the coolest rock group in the world. When you walk in my bedroom, the first thing you see is a six-foot color poster of lead guitarist Jimmy Page. What do you think about that?"

"Are you a Christian?" I asked.

"Sure," he answered, almost defiantly.

"Well, then," I went on. "when people come into your room, who do they think is the most important person in your life, Jimmy Page or Jesus Christ?"

I stared him straight in the eye. "A week ago I might not have had the moral authority to tell you what I'm about to say, but I've just done something to make certain Jesus is head of my home. If Christ is really first in your life, tear that poster down today!"

You can't always be that blunt with teenagers, but there are times when they need to hear it straight from the shoulder. For you teenagers who are reading this book, there is one message you should get clearly. *If you want God to bless you, get the cursed things out of your life.*

"But it's just one poster of David Bowie. It's just one Aerosmith album. You don't think just one record will hurt me spiritually, do you?" you argue in defense.

Galatians 5:9 says, "A little leaven leaventh the whole lump."

As long as you tolerate even the slightest sin and inconsistency in your life, the devil has a toehold. In Joshua 7 we read that the sin of one man brought defeat upon Israel. Achan kept in his possession those things which God had cursed. The result was disaster and death for the entire nation.

The Enemy only needs one area of your life not committed to Christ to have access to the whole. Maybe that poster or record isn't an avenue of evil to hinder you spiritually, but what if it is? Is it worth it to hang on to that which may be cursed, lest you become like it?

You're probably still wondering what became of that dream

house. Well, it's still there looking as beautiful as ever. But right across the road from it stands another home that is even more magnificent. Nestled among some tall Ponderosa pines, it's the perfect hideaway for solitude and seclusion. The natural cedar wood exterior blends quietly into the surroundings. Outside the front door, squirrels scurry about, unmolested by traffic and the hazards of civilization. From the back porch you can look across a mountain valley on a warm summer evening and watch a herd of elk grazing in the meadow.

Even more so than the house that was almost ours, this is the kind of home that Kathy and I would treasure as a gift from God. And we do, because it's ours!

How did we come to build our real dream home right across the road from the house denied us because of obedience to parental authority?

Well, would you believe me if I told you that through a series of circumstances, the Lord showed us the actual design we should choose? Could you accept the fact that after several frustrating attempts to find a contractor, the Lord led us to the right man? He had just finished building and was planning to build again the very home the Lord had shown us three months earlier in an architectural book.

If you can't believe that, then you'd be amazed to hear of a dozen other details in both the construction and planning of our home that bore the stamp of God's miraculous intervention. It's not the world's most lavish and magnificent building, and it's not a mansion worthy of a millionaire or a king. But there is something special about that house. It's the home God wanted us to have.

If you were to drive out West and stop in Denver, there's something about our new home we'd want you to see. When you'd walk in the front door, you couldn't help but notice the sign we have hanging there. It has one word on it: Shamea. That's Hebrew for "to be obedient." Down in the corner is a Scripture reference, Isaiah 1:19: "If ye be willing and obedient, ye shall eat the good of the land."

GLOSSARY OF ROCK GROUPS

Just about the time a parent thinks he has mastered a vague
understanding of the rock scene, the kids come up with their
favorite tactic: "Why can't I listen to such-and-such rock group?
They aren't homosexuals, they don't use drugs, and they
don't sing about sex. Can I buy one of their albums?"

Now, what can a parent do? You've never even heard of the
group in question and have no idea whether they're offensive or
acceptable. There's no way you can stay informed enough
on this subject to outmaneuver your children. You don't want to
be unreasonably restrictive, but neither do you want to
expose your family to the influence of negative moral philosophies.

The following glossary of popular music groups has been
compiled with this dilemma in mind. Please understand that it
would be impossible to devise an exhaustive list of every
band on the charts. Therefore, you will find cited only the better
known groups which have had the highest record sales in
recent years. Some groups which have been discussed earlier in
the book are not mentioned again. Others which were
covered only in passing have been analyzed further in this
glossary.

What if your children bring up a name that is not included? It
might be that the group or person came on the scene after
the publication date of this book, or rose to fame after we went to
press. There are thousands of singers and musicians with

the potential of stardom and covering every band would be an impossible task.

Consequently, this glossary can't give all the answers. It will provide some valuable insights regarding the major names in the rock entertainment industry. Hopefully, the group your children ask about will be listed. If not, the basic guidelines already expressed in this book should give you something to go on.

Remember as you read what follows that Jesus Christ loves the sex-obsessed rock star as much as he does you and your child. Christ is not willing that any should perish (2 Pet. 3:9), and that includes KISS and Cooper. Approaching this glossary on that basis will help you to interpret the information in a constructive manner.

Some might ask why it is necessary to discuss in such intimate detail the immoral views of these individuals. Because of who they are, the way they live is a matter of public record. Most knowledgeable young people are aware of such information. It is parents who need to be "educated" on this subject as they can make intelligent decisions as to what images their children should not be allowed to emulate.

Others may feel the analyses are slanted toward bringing out the negative aspects of rock artists without fairly drawing attention to more positive elements in their character and music. It should be obvious that what's good isn't a problem and doesn't need accentuation. The glossary is not intended as a "fair" appraisal of all that an entertainer stands for. It is the objectionable moral impact of these people with which we're concerned, and that is why this aspect is emphasized.

1. ABBA
2. Aerosmith
3. Beachboys
4. The Beatles
5. Bee Gees
6. Black Sabbath
7. Blue Oyster Cult
8. Boston
9. Bowie, David
10. Clapton, Eric

11. Cooper, Alice
12. Emerson, Lake, and Palmer
13. Frampton, Peter
14. The Grateful Dead
15. Jefferson Starship
16. Jethro Tull
17. John, Elton
18. KISS
19. Led Zeppelin
20. Nugent, Ted
21. Presley, Elvis
22. Queen
23. The Rolling Stones
24. Stewart, Rod
25. The Who

ABBA

Little-known in America, the Swedish quartet, ABBA, has swept the rest of the world. As Sweden's most profitable corporation, they surpass Volvo with earnings of $12 million a year. Even Russians pay $130 on the black market for an ABBA album. High taxes in their native, socialistic country have driven their financial conglomerate to collect payment in services and goods such as grain and oil. The name ABBA is an anagram of the four members of the group, and their music is predictable, styled to appeal to a middle-of-the-road pop audience. One couple of the group, married since 1971, have finally divorced. The other pair, keyboardist, Benny Anderson, and singer, Anni-Fried Lyngstad, continue to live together in open fornication, a so-called "Stockholm marriage." While their music and most of their lyrics may be blandly unobjectionable, the life styles they flaunt make the purchase of an ABBA album a possible subsidy of public promiscuity.

AEROSMITH

The soft sounds of the seventies did little to deter this hard-driving Boston band. Their albums sell into the millions, and one of

them, "Toys in the Attic," was on the charts for 150 weeks.
Faithful audiences of up to 80,000 come to hear them churn out
deafening metal sounds and profane lyrics. The main focus
of the group is on its androgynous lead singer, Steve Tyler. A
pedometer has clocked his stage movements during a concert
for a total of four miles per performance. Tyler croons
of the cheerleader who was a "young bleeder" and the short-
skirted girl with a "kitty in the middle." His fantasies were
apparently fulfilled with Cyrinda Fox, whom he married
after she became pregnant with his child. When police busted
fifty-two young people at one of their concerts, Aerosmith
paid $3,650 to bail out the drug offenders. Tyler boasts of his own
arrest for drugs while in the eleventh grade. The assault
this band makes on the ears of their fans is doubly objectionable
for its morality as well as its decibels.

BEACHBOYS

While most sixties groups faded with the onslaught of psychedelia,
the Beachboys survived both musical and personal changes.
The all-American California surfers delved into LSD (Brian
Wilson), flirtation with the Manson Family (Dennis Wilson), and
transcendental meditation (Mike Love and Al Jardine). But
they survived as a unit to excite a whole new generation of rock
fans to whom they were old enough to be fathers. Their durability
and close harmonies sold 80 million records in their first
fifteen years together. While their early songs may have been
innocuous tributes to high school pursuits, their personal
involvement in more serious matters of life has undoubtedly
influenced many. The Christian teenager who nostalgically
bounces to "Surfin U.S.A." should remember that the fame of the
Beachboys was a launching pad for the Maharishi Mahesh Yogi's
introduction of TM and occultic mysticism into the mainstream
of America.

THE BEATLES

Why analyze a group that no longer exists? Because the Beatles
endure through their music, and as Shakespeare put it,
"The evil that men do lives on after them." What the Beatles said

in the sixties set the tone for topics as diverse as drugs, war, parents, and respect for authority. Their melodies have melted into our consciousness (where would Muzak be without "Yesterday" and "Michelle"?), but their lyrics and life styles brought about a revolution. The Fabulous Four altered society's perception of public decency forever. The erotic escapades of John and Yoko, the glorification of drug experimentation via "I Get High with a Little Help from My Friends," and the Beatles' espousal of TM affected the values of millions. Though "I Want to Hold Your Hand" may pale by comparison to Rod Stewart's "Do Ya Think I'm Sexy," John, Paul, George, and Ringo taught us to accept pop idols as arbiters of sex, politics, and religion. The Beatles may have been only temporarily "more popular than Jesus," but it was long enough to alter the music and morals of the Western world.

BEE GEES

Barry, Robin, and Maurice Gibb, better known as the Bee Gees (brothers Gibb), achieved a domination of the pop charts not seen since the days of the Beatles. With the help of *Saturday Night Fever*, the movie for which they penned the tunes, they were expected to gross $210 million in one year. After an early string of sixties hits, the brothers fell into a period of drugs and division. The album, "Main Course," containing a song based on the name of an evil spirit ("Shenandorah"), marked a turning point in their careers. With the help of the disco craze and a return to concentration on falsetto harmonies, the Bee Gees found a new following and fame. At one point, half of the Top Ten hits belonged to them, bringing their No. 1 hit totals to the largest of any artist or group of the seventies. Though their public image exudes wholesomeness, interviews on their private lives revealed them to be less than paragons of virtue.[1] Robin confesses to a hobby of pornographic drawings, and all three lace their comments with obscenities. Barry insists that the album, "Spirits Having Flown," is infiltrated with references to reincarnation, while Maurice and Robin lay claim to the psychic powers of E.S.P. Such occultic fascination, coupled with a propensity for perverse language, make their hit, "Too Much Heaven," sound like a contradiction of interests, as well as destinations.

[1]*Rolling Stone,* May 17, 1979.

BLACK SABBATH

Their music is called by some "Satan rock," and they have been known (for publicity purposes) to hold black masses before a concert (complete with a nude on an altar sprinkled with chicken blood). Their first album pictured the cross of Christ upside down. A later album, "Sabbath, Bloody Sabbath," depicted a nude satanic ritual with the numbers 666 emblazoned across the front. Associations like this made their choice of the name, Black Sabbath, seem more than appropriate. Their aggressive, belligerent, heavy-metal music, droning lyrics, and blast-furnace bass lines fit the image their public relations men hope to convey. Bumper stickers declare, "I'm possessed by Black Sabbath," and fan club T-shirts display a skull-and-crossbones with the Antichrist's numbered designation, 666.

As their popularity grew, the band sought to shed their earlier black magic image. Still, one rock periodical says, "They demonstrate an almost hellish power over the audience."[1] Several members of the group admit to involvement in astral projection, and lead singer Ozzy Osbourne claims he was compelled to see *The Exorcist* twenty-six times.[2] Osbourne says, "I don't know if I'm a medium for some outside force. Whatever it is, frankly, I hope it's not what I think—Satan."[3] The demonic overtones of this British band may be contrived to sell records. But it is well to remember that when men use satanic symbols even in jest, the devil takes such dabbling seriously.

[1]*Circus,* February, 1976, p. 60.
[2]*Ibid.,* April 22, 1976, p. 35.
[3]*Hit Parader,* February, 1978, p. 24.

BLUE OYSTER CULT

With a name like Blue Oyster Cult, what could be expected? As America's answer to Black Sabbath, their songs live up

to their sinister-sounding title. "Don't Fear the Reaper"
counseled a love pact of teenage suicide. "Tenderloin" describes
the gay district of San Francisco, and "E.T.I." was dedicated
to the belief in extraterrestrial intelligences. The strange,
occult-like symbol that adorns their records has yet to be
deciphered, adding to the mystery of their image. In concert,
their haunting lyrics are accompanied by a laser light show that
has been labeled by the Food and Drug Administration as
visually dangerous to concert-goers. With their heavy-metal
sounds and sadistic-leather overtones, perhaps the same
should be said of their music.

BOSTON

For hard-rockers who lamented the popularity of disco and
softer sounds, Boston was a welcome, if not deafening, sonic relief.
Led by twenty-nine-year-old M.I.T. graduate, Tom Scholz,
Boston's first album soared from obscurity to sell three-and-a-half
million copies, riding to success on their initial hit, "More
Than a Feeling." Boston triggers enthusiastic audience response
by asking for marijuana joints as a prelude to their tune
"Smokin'." Scholz, who worked in the research and development
division of Polaroid, has been described as a genius of electronic
wizardry. Their overpowering concerts would seem the
perfect place to market the ultimate ear plug, if Scholz could
add such a device to his catalogue of inventions.

BOWIE, DAVID

As the first pop music star to openly proclaim his homosexuality,
David Bowie set the stage for other artists to come out of
the closet. His wife, Angela, was kicked out of Connecticut
College for being a lesbian. The two met, *People* magazine
reported, while they were involved with the same man.[1] Bowie
has also confessed to a deep involvement in drugs from heroin to
cocaine. He admits, "Actually, I was junked out of my mind
most of the time. You can do good things with drugs, but then
comes the long decline."[2] Ironically, Bowie has this to say
of the medium that propelled his rise to stardom: "Rock and roll
has always been the devil's music. It could well bring about

a very evil feeling in the West."[3] References to decadence in his
songs and performances would be too numerous to mention.
Perhaps his own flaunting of perversion is what led Bowie to finally
conclude, "I've never been in love. Love is a disease that
breeds jealousy, anxiety, and brute anger."[4]

[1]*People*, August 18, 1975, p. 68.
[2]*Rolling Stone*, January 12, 1978, p. 13.
[3]*Ibid.*, February 12, 1976, p. 83.
[4]*Ibid.*, February 12, 1976, p. 80.

CLAPTON, ERIC

Eric Clapton has been recognized by many as the most
accomplished guitarist of his generation. With groups like Cream,
he established himself as one of the first true "superstar"
musicians. A later fall into heroin addiction (which he treated with
acupuncture) brought about a period of decline. Of his bout
with drugs, Clapton says, "I had my first taste and thought, oh,
you know, one snort can't do me any harm. But...dead
wrong!"[1] A brief commitment to Christ, from which he later
turned, resulted in his writing "In the Presence of the Lord."

[1]*Rolling Stone*, July 18, 1974, p. 54.

COOPER, ALICE

Vincent Furnier, the preacher's son from Arizona, rose to fame
as Alice Cooper by giving his fans exhibitions of transvestitism,
snakes, mutilated chickens, and mock public executions. His
record albums were each based on unified concepts exploring
ever-deepening stages of perversion. "School's Out" featured its
vinyl encased in disposable women's panties. "Billion Dollar
Babies" pictured a baby made up with Cooper-style mascara.
"Muscle of Love" extolled the pleasures of masturbation.
"Welcome to My Nightmare" was staged by Alice simulating sex
with a corpse via a lifelike-looking mannequin, and "Alice
Cooper Goes to Hell" suggested the rouge-rock queen ultimately
meets up with the devil who is characterized as "the greatest,
number one."

Such outrages brought Cooper immense wealth and ultimate

respectability. After turning the stomachs and minds of fifteen-year-olds, Alice unleashed his lewd theatrics on adult Tahoe casino-goers who shelled out $15 each. As even more violent and shocking acts came upon the scene (e.g., KISS), Alice, who had once declared, "No more Mr. Nice Guy," sought refuge among Hollywood's in-crowd. He played golf with George Burns and helped rebuild the city's crumbling hillside sign. Cooper's ambi-sexual horror shows finally resulted in a desperate bout with alcoholism. Though he once credited his fame to the possession of a spirit from a seventeenth-century witch, Alice found age and physical exhaustion catching up with his image. In the wake of his past were the lives of thousands of impressionable teens who found in Alice Cooper a rationale for rebellion. Many of his fans have likely explored the perversions he had parodied.

EMERSON, LAKE & PALMER

Three musicians, thirty-two tons of equipment, and 72,000 watts of amplification comprise this British superstar trio. Carl Palmer's customized drum set is worth $50,000, and Keith Emerson insists that every hotel room on tour come complete with his own electric piano for spontaneous improvisations. Their combination of "rockified" classics and romantic ballads was performed on one tour with the help of a sixty-four-piece orchestra. Such virtuosity was augmented by Emerson's stunt of pummeling his piano with daggers while it is hydraulically hoisted into midair for the finale. As the instrument rotates above the stage, Emerson pounds out the final chords just before the ivories literally burst into flames. Such expensive, outlandish theatrics comprise the kind of show that only a pampered, materialistic generation would cheer to see.

FRAMPTON, PETER

After years of playing for lesser groups and smaller fees, Peter Frampton burst on the scene with one album that generated $50 million income over a twelve-month period. His baby-faced image was deliberately promoted to evoke sensuality, such as the legs-wide-apart pose for the cover of his second solo album.

Frampton admits that the sudden rise to stardom put such
pressure on him that he turned to alcohol to cope with the whole
scene. Such success was short-lived as Peter failed to follow
through on his meteoric career. Rock fans are fickle, and
today's star very quickly becomes a has-been if his future
commercial offerings are not accepted by the buying public.

THE GRATEFUL DEAD

Standing next to Jefferson Starship as the Frisco band who best
symbolizes the era of flower-power is The Grateful Dead.
Early on, lead guitarist Jerry Garcia declared, "Acid rock is music
you listen to when you are high on acid."[1] Their concerts
are frequented by faithful legions of "dead-heads" whose
attendance is marked as much by drugs as it is by the music. They
sport the world's largest sound system—190 speaker cabinets
—to convey the rhythms of their tripping-out chords. Age and
affluence have mellowed the group little, as evidenced by the
recent drug conviction of Garcia for possession of LSD,
pot, and cocaine. Ron ("Pigpen") McKernan, considered by some
the band's most creative musician, died from the self-destructive
accumulation of alcohol and drugs. The message seems lost
on those remaining. "Our lives are controlled by music," Garcia
concedes.[2]

[1]*Rolling Stone*, February 3, 1972, p. 30.
[2]*People*, July 12, 1976, p. 50.

JEFFERSON STARSHIP

The shrill vocals of Grace Slick and the flower-power of the Haight
Asbury era gave birth to this early acid-rock, Frisco band.
They began by singing the glories of drugs ("White Rabbit") and
violent revolution ("Volunteers"), and they lived what they
sang. Members of the band were repeatedly arrested for drug
usage, causing lead guitarist Paul Kanter to comment, "The group
paid for it [the drugs], it was a business expense."[1] Grace
Slick bore an illegitimate child and disdained marriage by
commenting, "A lot of our generation is lazy, they'd rather sit
around and smoke dope than go down to the courthouse and
fill out a lot of papers."[2] Blasphemy was their bag too, as evidenced

in the album, "Long John Silver," which descri[...]
as a bastard having an affair with Mary Magdalen[...]

As the years rolled on, the group's name changed fr[...]
Airplane to Jefferson Starship, and their interest mov[...]
from drugs to mysticism. They retained an acupunctur[...]
relieve tensions, explored oriental philosophy, and sang
UFOs ("Song to the Sun"). Guitarist Craig Chaquico obse[...]
"Rock concerts are the churches of today. Music puts them
on a spiritual plane. All music is God."[3] Despite these alteration[...]
Slick continued her drug-bent ways, although motherhood did
slow down her doping somewhat. "It's hard to keep an eye on the
kid while you're hallucinating," she admitted.[4] Her ultimate
nemesis was alcohol. The bottle forced her to split from the group,
and the Starship's flight potential without Grace was questionable.
Few other rock bands reflect so well the flow of the counter-
culture, from early days of hippiedom in the sixties to the
narcissistic hedonism of the seventies.

[1]*Rolling Stone*, September 30, 1971, p. 30.
[2]*Newsweek*, March 16, 1971.
[3]*Bay Area Music Magazine*, February 1, 1977.
[4]*People*, August 28, 1978, p. 72.

JETHRO TULL

With a name derived from an eighteenth-century agriculturalist
who invented the seed drill, this British band charted the
more musically sophisticated end of the rock spectrum. Led by
talented flutist, Ian Anderson, their stage performances
are loaded with provocative vulgarities. Anderson plays while
bouncing up and down on one leg, his wild hair flung to
the wind and his wild eyes dancing. He obscenely gestures,
putting his flute to his crotch nearly as often as to his mouth.
Tull's lyrical topics have ranged from blasphemous attacks
on Christ ("Aqualung") to a dead ballerina ("A Passion Play,"
which also has sacrilegious references to the Father and Son
—G. Oddie Snr. and G. Oddie Jnr.). Such comments are
not merely incidental. Anderson once planned a movie in which
he'd play God. He theorizes, "If Jesus Christ came back
today, He and I would get into our brown corduroys and go to the

...e and overturn the racks of blue denim. ...crucified in the morning."[1]

...e, March 10, 1977, p. 13.

..., ELTON

...current popularity of the piano as a rock instrument owes its ...surgence to the talent of one man: Elton John. Noted for ...his musical genius and clever melodies, John has sung of topics as diverse as lesbianism ("All the Young Girls Love Alice") and glue sniffing ("The Bitch is Back"). His annual income of $7 million has supported outlandish fetishes such as feathered boas and 200 pairs of glasses worth $40,000. One set has eighty-seven light bulbs that spell out his name. His father quotes him as saying, "It's all a big con. But as long as the public laps it up, I'm quite happy to go on giving it to them."[1] While John may be respected for his technical brilliance with the piano, his moral views are less shining. He admits to being both suicidal and bisexual. "I crave to be loved," he told *Rolling Stone* magazine. "There's nothing wrong with going to bed with somebody of your own sex. I just think people should be very free with sex—they should draw the line at goats."[2]

[1]*Rolling Stone*, July 15, 1976, p. 30.
[2]*Ibid.*, October 7, 1976, p. 17.

KISS

What Alice Cooper was to dead babies and corpses, KISS became to fire-breathing and sadomasochism. With Kubuki-whitened faces, they leap on stage puking blood, declaring, "God of rock and roll, we'll steal your virgin soul." Producer Bob Ezrin described KISS as "symbols of unfettered evil and sensuality."[1] Their leather-gay costuming and flair for stage violence earned the group a fanatical following, referred to as their "army." Rock magazines call them "fire-breathing demons from rock and roll hell." Gene Simmons of the band is best known for his ability to lasciviously extend his tongue, an ancient pagan symbol of demon worship. On the liner notes for one album jacket,

Simmons describes his love techniques of "d.
things that make you writhe and groan in ecsta

Not satisfied with their erotic image, band mem
more satanic overtones. Peter Criss boldly declare.
myself evil. I believe in the devil as much as God.
either one to get things done."[3] Gene Simmons, who
an interest in cannibalism, adds, "If God is hot stuff, w
He afraid to have other gods before Him? I've always wan
to be God."[4]

Their depravity seems to know no end. The album, "Love
Gun," contained a song dedicated to "Plaster Casters," rock music
prostitutes (groupies) who make plaster of paris replicas of the
genitals of famous rock stars. Marvel Comics produced a
special edition dedicated to KISS. Blood samples were taken from
the group and smeared on the plates so they could literally
say the comic was printed in the blood of the band. Marvel editor,
Steve Gerber, deliberately aimed the magazine at eight- to
nine-year-olds, stating that the decadence of KISS would enhance
sales because the band appeals to "the baser qualities of
human nature." Gerber adds, "At first the parents' reaction
will be total revulsion. Then they'll just shake their heads
in dismay and go back to watching T.V."[5] The KISS comic was
the biggest selling one in history.

Marvel's success has blossomed into a small industry of KISS
paraphernalia including jeans, dolls, Halloween costumes,
eyeshadow, shampoo, soap, cologne, necklaces, hats, and belt
buckles. The expected gross for one year is $117 million.
A television special featured the group exhibiting psychic
phenomena, enlarging their boundaries of power to the supernatural.

Whether their demented demeanor evokes images of sensuality
(Simmons claims to have slept with 1,000 women.[6]), or
violence, their psychodramas are emulated by millions of teens.
Several who copied Simmons' fire-breathing exhibition have
suffered serious burns. One young fan killed a classmate who had
quarreled with him over KISS. Steve Glantz, a Detroit rock
promoter, said of them, "It's almost like Hitler-rock because that
audience—because of their beat, they're mesmerized by
the music. They have that audience hypnotized. They could say,
'We're going out there and lift up this building,' and they'd
just lift it up. That's the kind of control they have."[7]

rch 25, 1976, p. 9.
, 1976, p. 20.
1977, p. 49.
ember 13, 1976, p. 42.
ntain News, April 26, 1977.
May 22, 1978, p. 124.
, April 8, 1976, p. 27.

.D ZEPPELIN

As rock entered into its third decade and matured as a musical force by mellowing and encompassing self-conscious sophistication, one band continued to top the charts and set stadium attendance records with hard-driving sounds. Led Zeppelin kept their heavy core of raw rock, though they could turn partially pensive with tunes like "Stairway to Heaven," a rock classic that has been voted the most popular tune of rock's history. Their lyrics have been both visionary and sexual from "Whole Lotta Love," with unrepeatable references, to "Black Dog," which describes his lover's "honey drip." Lead guitarist Jimmy Page explains, "Rock and roll is [sexual expletive]-you music."[1]

Led Zeppelin is known as much for their swinging concert tours as their music. Transported across the country in a $2,500-per-hour chartered jet (complete with sauna, library, art gallery, video tape monitors, and a gourmet food gallery), they have earned a reputation for outlandish antics. In one Hollywood hotel, they destroyed paintings, submerged four stereos in bathtubs, and held motorcycle races in the hallways. Other tales include one rock magazine's account of a groupie (rock prostitute) they doused with a bucket of urine and another girl who was tied to a bed with fresh fish jammed into her orifices.[2] Such tales of perversity may seem unnecessarily blunt to some, but perhaps it's time teenage rock fans realized what unthinkable debauchery is being financed by the concert tickets they purchase.

The group's preoccupation with zaniness is less frightening than their flirtation with the occult. Lead singer Robert Plant admits to a fascination with black magic, but can hardly hold a candle to the occultic interests of guitarist Jimmy Page. He owns the admittedly demon-possessed home of the late satanist, Aleister Crowley, and runs his own occult bookshop

because, he explains, "There was not one good collection of books
on the occult in London and I was tired of having to go all
different places to get the books I wanted."[3] To charges that he is
a practicing witch, Page answers somewhat unconvincingly,
"I do not worship the devil. But magic does intrigue me."[4]
Zeppelin's album, "Presence," displayed an oddly shaped object
that has stirred speculation as to its meaning. Page reveals
that its design is supposed to symbolize the force that enables the
group to so profoundly affect audiences, a power that is simply
referred to as a "presence."[5] Such revelations leave one
wondering if Led Zeppelin's enduring popularity might be at least
partially attributable to something more than the mind-boggling,
heavy-metal sounds that churn forth from their amps.

Circus, June 23, 1977, p. 35.
Ibid., October, 1973, p. 69.
Hit Parader, July, 1975, p. 64.
Ibid.

NUGENT, TED

Billing himself as "the guitar gunslinger," Ted Nugent makes no
attempt to placate those who want subtle sophistication in
their pop music. He calls his music "combat rock," which involves
a barrage of feedback and stage acrobatics, including Nugent's
leap from atop amplifiers while clad only in a loin cloth.
His pornographic lyrics are accompanied by guitar riffs that are
amplified far beyond the threshold of pain. Nugent has
taken to performing with earplugs but allows no such consideration for his audiences. Describing his outlook on rock, he
declares, "Rock is a perfect primal method of releasing our violent
instincts. I used to rape [an audience], now I like a little
foreplay. I literally demand a reaction from an audience."[1] He
apparently gets what he wants. A rock periodical reported
that twelve people died in a riot after a performance in South
Carolina.[2] As rock's ignoble savage, Ted will have no trouble
keeping his image as the Motor City Madman.

Circus, May 13, 1976, p. 29.
Ibid.

PRESLEY, ELVIS

The outlandish stage antics of today's rock groups are possible because one man broke down the moral barriers of public entertainment. That man, known for a gyrating pelvis and lewd gesticulations, was Elvis Presley. So great was the influence of "the King," that after his death fans marched on Washington insisting his birthday be declared a national holiday. Various magazines quoted friends and confidants as revealing that Elvis was addicted to a variety of drugs, including heroin. A bodyguard claimed the buttocks of Elvis were so pocketed with needle marks there was hardly room left for an injection. The man who fervently sang "He Touched Me" and "How Great Thou Art" finally reached the state, we are told, in which it was impossible to eat, sleep, or sing without the aid of pills.

Some also claimed Elvis entertained a morose interest in the occult. He studied paranormal phenomena and communicated regularly with a psychic in Denver, Colorado. Elvis claimed he could form clouds with the power of his mind and would sometimes load friends into his limousine for a midnight visit to the coroner or the graveyard. In fact, one close friend contended that Elvis actually believed he was Jesus with the power to draw out diseases by his hands.

From a $35-a-week truck driver to singer with an amassed career income of $4.3 billion, Elvis captured the heart of America like no other popular entertainer before or since. On the way, he turned from an Assembly of God choirboy into a devotee of the Hindu mystic, Paramahansa Yogananda, founder of the Self-Realization Fellowship. Though some prominent preachers insisted Elvis had made it to heaven, the only certainty seemed to be that calories and chemicals had ended a career unparalleled in entertainment history.

QUEEN

"We want to shock and be outrageous," says lead singer Freddie Mercury,[1] and the choice of their name with its gay-drag overtones is a good place to start. On stage, Mercury sports heavy mascara, purple fingernail polish, and strips to the hot pants that are underneath his tight, satin clothing to further promote the group's bisexual ambivalence. Queen lyrics range from the unprintable sexual solicitation of "Get Down, Make Love" to the blasphemous chorus "All going down to see the Lord Jesus." Their LP, "Jazz," was promoted by Queen's sponsorship of a nude bicycle race featuring fifty-five undraped entrants. For two hours, Mercury struts his stuff, whipping concert audiences into a frenzy with his erotic body contortions. Little wonder that their song, "We Are the Champions," has been widely interpreted as an anthem of gay liberation. "On stage, I am a devil," Freddie admits. "I think I may go mad in several years' time."[2] In calmer moments, the group insists that it's all an act, a contrivance to draw the crowds. But illusion and reality can affect both a culture's values as well as the morals of the teen record-buyer who fails to see beyond Queen's pornographic parodies.

[1]*Circus,* April, 1974, p. 41.
[2]*Ibid.,* March 17, 1977, p. 42.

THE ROLLING STONES

The names of most rock groups are like foreign appellations to most adults. But there does not breathe a parent who would remain bewildered at the mention of the Rolling Stones, and every negative and repulsive connotation the group has assiduously cultivated would immediately come to mind. Though somewhat tempered by acceptance and affluence, their early image of savagery, evil, and rebellion has remained intact, thanks to press coverage of Keith Richards' heroin bust and Mick Jagger's promiscuous meanderings. Richards admits, "There are black magicians who think we are acting as unknown agents of Lucifer."[1] To support such speculation, the Stones' songs have ranged from the espousal of violent revolution in "Street Fighting Man" to the anthem of satanists, "Sympathy for the Devil." The death of four fans at the fateful Altamount rock fest sealed for good their image as purveyors of the sinister.

A Stones concert is an orgy of sexual celebration with Jagger as the head cheerleader. Strutting and prancing across the stage, his androgynous performances evoke the delight of both men and women. On one tour his mascara-laden playacting concluded with a giant balloon in the shape of a male phallus rising up out of the stage. "Sometimes, being on stage is better than an orgasm," Jagger acknowledges.[2] Reports have regularly circulated in the press that Jagger and his estranged wife, Bianca (who insists most of her friends are gay), are both bisexual. One story even had a Jagger-David Bowie relationship breaking up the latter's marriage. True or not, such speculation is all part of the debaucherous aura surrounding Mick's role as rock's icon of demonism. He does admit that his first sexual experience was homosexual and confesses a desire for his own daughter to have sex "at an early age."[3]

As the enduring, aging, multi-millionaires of rock, the Stones continue to convey lawless outrage all the while they cavort with the Establishment of high society and seek for tax shelters. Their proclivity for sexual explicitness that shocked fans a decade earlier, hardly raises a blush today. When they urinated on the streets of London in the sixties, a stunned public declared them offensive. Today, their overindulgence in cocaine and sadomasochism is chic at its best and barely titillating at its worst.

Keith Richards once observed that the Stones' songs come spontaneously, like inspiration "at a seance." He explains that the tunes arrive "en masse," as if the Stones, as songwriters, were only a willing and open "medium."[4] With voodoo incantations and the screams of demon possession accompanying cuts like "Dancing with Mr. D" (the devil), one is left wondering if perhaps the satanic imagery of Mr. Jagger and company is all concocted. One thing is certain, their fans aren't the only victims. As Jagger expresses the frustrations of stardom and sensual satiation in their hit, "Shattered," he concludes that fame and fortune have left him in tatters. After working to achieve "success and sex," he asks, "Does it matter?"

[1]*Rolling Stone*, August 19, 1971.
[2]*Ibid.*, July 17, 1975, p. 37.
[3]*People*, October 3, 1977, p. 108.
[4]*Rolling Stone*, May 5, 1977, p. 55.

STEWART, ROD

Mention the name Rod Stewart, and the average rock fan will think of Rod's love life as much as his music. The latter has been heavily laden with erotic overtones from "Tonight's the Night" (in which he requests his angel to "spread" her wings so he can "come inside"), to "Hot Legs" ("Hot legs keep my pencil sharp."). His first big hit, "Maggie May," was addressed to a lover who would wreck his bed after she "wore him out." When questioned about his heavy makeup and fey-oriented performances, he adds, "I always wanted to be attractive to men. That's half the people who buy our records."[1] In real life Stewart has been linked with a bevy of luscious women, though he concedes he takes Vitamin E to keep up with his rapacious sex life. "A happy home life, security, and in-laws aren't conducive to making rock and roll," he concluded.[2] Alana Hamilton finally married Rod, though she had to walk to the altar pregnant to succeed where Britt Ekland had failed. Rod Stewart has proven that sex sells records and that an artist's reputation for fornication can be as important in maintaining stardom as the musical efforts that originally gained him notoriety.

[1]*Rolling Stone*, June 21, 1973, p. 39.
[2]*Circus*, October 17, 1978, p. 36.

THE WHO

"Tommy" and The Who are thought of almost simultaneously, the former being the latter's ambitious rock opera that spawned an Ann Margret movie. As a metaphoric mockery of Christ, "Tommy" depicted everything from a surreal crucifixion to a vivid child molestation scene ("Lift up the nightshirt and fiddle Uncle Ernie."). The spiritual and musical mentor of the group, Peter Townshend, is known for his wildly atavistic stage act and espousal of eastern mysticism via the teachings of Meher Baba. In the early days, The Who were known for setting off smoke bombs (a common rock routine today) and smashing their instruments to smithereens at the end of a performance. On one tour they inflicted $30,000 worth of damages on a Holiday Inn to celebrate the drummer's birthday. The object of festivity, Keith Moon, carried a hatchet in his luggage to chop up the furniture of motel rooms when he felt bored.

Townshend mellowed with his devotion to Baba. A solo album dedicated to his guru contained songs extolling reincarnation, and a final tune adapted from the Baba's Hindu prayer, "Parvardigar."

Peter declares, "Baba is Christ," because being a Christian is "just like being a Baba lover."[1] On one occasion he described a frightening encounter with demonic powers. While contemplating the Hindu "Om" chant, he entered a trance state which precipitated an out-of-the-body experience. Townshend claims to have heard "the Niagran roar of a billion humans screaming,"[2] quite possibly a revelation of hell's tormented.

Lead singer Roger Daltry also played the messianic lead role of "Tommy" in the film version. His personal life style is somewhat less religious. He informs his wife of promiscuous dalliances while on the road, confessing, "When you're in a hotel, a pretty young lady makes life bearable."[3] His 200-acre Sussex estate includes an eight-foot replica of a genital, a prop from a film in which he starred.

The most tragic chapter of Who's history was written by drummer Keith Moon. His craziness was well chronicled—from the human excrement in his own living room to episodes of public exposure. Once he brushed death by driving a Lincoln Continental into a swimming pool. Moon was known to take up to twenty-five amphetamines at a time. Finally, an overdose of thirty-two antialcoholism tablets ended his life. Strangely enough, he had just finished recording the group's latest album, "Who Are You?" Had that question been personally answered by an understanding of God's purpose for his life, Moon's tragedy could have been averted.

[1]*Hit Parader*, March, 1972, p. 23.
[2]*Rolling Stone*, November 17, 1977, p. 55-56.
[3]*People*, December 13, 1975, p. 24.

ROCK UPDATE

A lot can happen in two years' time. That's especially true when it comes to changes in popular culture. Today's trend quickly becomes tomorrow's passing fad. Nowhere is this more apparent than in analyzing rock music. The first edition of this book was published in early 1980. Since then, heavies like Led Zeppelin have disbanded, disco has suffered a slow decline (forcing groups like the Village People to undergo a metamorphosis), and names like Van Halen, Journey, and AC/DC have surged to the foreground. Rock stardom is a fickle force that can suddenly catapult an artist to the heights of dizzying popularity (Pat Benatar) and then just as quickly let the bottom drop out (the Knack). What the capricious adulation of fans does not accomplish, economic recession and plunging concert ticket sales can. The only certainty is that rock's treatment of life and love will continue its moral decline.

ROCK AND SEX

"I'm a sex machine," sings Freddie Mercury of Queen ("Don't Stop Me Now"). Most rock stars echo that sentiment. Even more pop acts like The Captain and Tennille can't resist asking, "Do That to Me One More Time." To keep up with the times, "sweet and innocent" Olivia Newton John has issued an appeal to "get physical." When it comes to sexual overtones, Foreigner is hard to top. One of their album jackets features a frightened young girl seated in a male urinal. In "Women," Foreigner declares that the opposite sex belongs "in the back seat." "Dirty White Boy" is self-descriptive, and "Urgent" extols the virtues of quickie, self-gratifying sex "in the middle of the night." After all, the singer doesn't want "a love that will last," he only "needs it fast."

In the pop vein, Rupert Holmes's "Him" dealt with multiple lovers, and Linda Ronstadt asked bluntly, "How Do I Make You?" "Hot Rod Hearts" described two lovers "sweat shirt to sweater," a scene compatible with the graphic invitation issued by the Pointer Sisters who want a lover with a "Slow Hand." (The singer says she wants it "all night.") Ted Nugent sings about craving "Jail Bait" (sex with a thirteen-year-old) and adds, "My Love Is Like a Tire Iron" ("stiff as steel").

Her smash hit "Bette Davis Eyes" found Kim Carnes describing a lady who could "roll you like . . . dice." Rod Stewart explicitly brushed off any thought of meaningful relationships by craving only "Passion" on "one hot night" with a "stranger." Rock was raised in an era of ambiguity when groping in the back seat had to be disguised with lyrics about kissing in the dark. But rock's mock innocence is gone. REO Speedwagon's album picturing a prostitute in a state of semi-undress (before-or-after) aptly states the lyrical affections of modern music: "Hi-Infidelity."

ROCK AND DRUGS

The toll continues. Rock's young die while the beat goes on. Since the original publication date of this book the list of those done in by booze and dope has added Michael Bloomfield (session blues guitarist—heroin); John Bonham (Led Zeppelin drummer—alcohol); Sid Vicious (Sex Pistols bass player who stabbed his girl friend and then killed himself—heroin); Bon Scott (AC/DC lead singer—alcohol). Sly Stone came close, but managed to survive repeated nose operations for cocaine snorting along with run-ins with angel dust.[1] Don Henley of the Eagles was arrested for possession of cocaine, marijuana, and Quaaludes.[2]

Perhaps most frightening is the way many rock stars continue to view drug usage so nonchalantly. "I take drugs to get in an unpleasant frame of mind and then try to find a catharsis for it. It's a self-sacrifice," brags David Weiss of the New Wave band Was (Was Not).[3] When he was arrested in Japan for possession of 7.7

ounces of marijuana, Paul McCartney shrugged off the incident by saying, "Marijuana isn't as dangerous as some people make it."[4] Rock musicians who use high-paid attorneys to beat their drug raps and spend thousands on operations and detoxification programs to patch up their bodies may consider themselves above the laws of men and the law of averages. But are they also above the laws of life and death? They owe their popularity to the patronage of young fans who have financed such "high" living. More responsible conduct and less casual public statements are the least that could be expected from those who have the custody of impressionable young minds.

ROCK AND THE OCCULT

To cite entertainers who have ventured into the occult reads like a Who's Who of rock's royalty (see chapter six). Elton John's lyricist, Bernie Taupin, decorates his walls with "satanic" art ("The occult fascinates me.")[5] Australian rocker Billy Thorpe released an LP entitled "Children of the Sun," a concept album about beings from another world who keep a close watch on earthlings. A German band went so far as to call itself Lucifer's Friend and offered fans "devilishly good rock and roll," calling its latest release "the demonic new album."[6] Todd Rundgren went from Egyptology (see page 42) to excessive indulgence of pot and the mystical ways of Sufism.[7] Rush, who have pictured inverted pentagrams on nearly every album jacket, feature songs like "Witch Hunt" and "Camera Eye" describing the ability via reincarnation to recall past lives.

Maurice White of Earth, Wind, and Fire (see page 42), confesses involvement in palmistry, astrology, reincarnation, Buddhism, TM, and UFO's. "It's all oneness, man," he explains. "I'm continuing a life from Atlantis [the lost land of occultists]. I have seen a couple of ghosts. They don't scare me... beings exist in other dimensions."[8]

Ritchie Blackmore (see page 41) has even changed the spelling of his first name to conform with numerological beliefs. He also acknowledges that he likes "ghost hunting" and has experienced supernatural demonic manifestations during seances. "Mental hospitals are full of people who are actually possessed by trouble-making spirits," he insists. Of his own black magic involvement he points out, "I must meet a hundred 'witches' a month. The real ones are reluctant to come forward with their stories. You can tell when they're sincere."[9]

PUNK/NEW WAVE

It started out in the mid-seventies with British youth who wore tattered clothes and jammed safety-pins through their noses. Dedicated to hate and nihilism, the Sex Pistols were the first major voice of Punk Rock, singing, "I am anti-Christ . . . an anarchist." Bands galore sprung up from seedy night spots to shock public sensibilities with grotesque names: the Castrators (an all-girl group); the Vibrators (whose dildo decadence spawned tunes in celebration of chains and razor blades); Blank Generation; Eddie and the Hot Rods (the album cover showed the drummer hanging himself); the Stranglers (who sang "Hangin' Around," mocking the Crucifixion).

Performers and audiences were caught up in a common identity and behavior characterized by self-mutilation, public profanity, and lots of spit and sweat. With no past to respect and no future to anticipate, punk rockers were the ultimate narcissists slam-dancing their way into the public's consciousness. (Slam-dancing is a bash-and-be-bashed dance technique of smashing violently into the nearest body which is also gyrating to high-powered Punk music.)

America didn't buy Punk at first until Southern California and the Northeast modified it to New Wave and doused it with speed and booze. Groups with some musical and intellectual capacities picked up the trend to bring back straight-ahead rock and roll. These include: Split Enz; the Police; the Talking Heads (a cut off of one album features a Katherine Kuhlman sermon); the B-52's (who dress as if they were caught in a fifties' time warp); the Psychedelic Furs (one member calls their music "beautiful chaos")[10]; Devo (whose trademark is wearing inverted flower pots on their heads); the Boomtown Rats (whose song "I Don't Like Monday" was inspired from a line uttered by a San Diego teenager who shot two men and wounded eight children); the Damned; the Dead Boys (whose lead singer stuffs Kotex in his pants, vomits beer, smashes his face into amplifiers, and dedicates a song to the mass murderer Richard Speck because "he knew what love is")[11]; and the Clash (whose album "Sandinista" was dedicated to Nicaraguan Communist guerrillas).

Though a few American rock fans entered the eighties still clinging to their orange hair, swastikas, dog collars, and self-destructive impulses, most preferred the more controlled rebellion of the Ramones, the Jam, the Vapors, and even the British "ska" sounds of the Specials and Bus Boys. After all, as Tommy Ramone put it, their music is basic rock and roll, "sexy, hard and violent," not progressive and polished.[12] Elvis Costello agrees, knocking more conventional rock bands like Boston by saying, "Rock and roll is about sex and they [Boston] might as well be eunuchs . . . I'm here to corrupt American youth."[13]

FOOTNOTES

[1]*People*, January 14, 1980, p. 30.

[2]*Rolling Stone*, April 2, 1981, p. 36.

[3]*Ibid.*, August 20, 1981, p. 10.

[4]*Ibid.*, March 6, 1980, p. 30.

[5]*People*, June 23, 1980.

[6]*Billboard*, July 5, 1980, p. 7.

[7]*Rolling Stone*, June 25, 1981, p. 49.

[8]*Crawdaddy*, February 1978, p. 18.

[9]*Circus*, April 30, 1981, pp. 45, 46.

[10]*Rolling Stone*, November 13, 1980, p. 28.

[11]*Billboard*, July 9, 1977, p. 38.

[12]*People*, January 3, 1977, p. 100.

[13]*Time*, May 8, 1978, p. 113.

* * *

ROCK

he following section is an updated *Rock* glossary. Several of the groups listed (indicated by an asterisk) have been previously covered. The reason for their inclusion here is to acquaint the reader with new, relevant information. Other groups not previously included in the glossary have been added because of their importance to rock's music and message.

1. AC/DC
2. Benetar, Pat
* 3. Black Sabbath
4. Blondie
* 5. Blue Oyster Cult
* 6. Fleetwood Mac
7. Journey
8. Judas Priest
* 9. Kiss
*10. Led Zeppelin
11. Ozzy Osbourne
12. Pink Floyd
13. Plasmatics
14. Pretenders, The
*15. Queen
*16. Rolling Stones, The
17. Springsteen, Bruce
18. Styx
19. Van Halen
*20. Who, The

AC/DC

With the turn into the eighties, five delinquents from down under showed America the firebrand hard rock that had already captivated the Aussies. "Dirty Deeds Done Dirt Cheap," their re-released '78 album said it all. Their "deeds" included lyrics and album graphics too explicit for this book to quote. Even the mentionables are appalling. Song titles include, "Big Balls," "Love at First Feel," "Let Me Put My Love into You," and "Highway to Hell." The last mentioned tune was delivered with a lascivious growl by lead singer Bon Scott. With a direct lyrical invitation for Satan to claim his soul, Scott declared hell to be the "promised land" and warned that nothing would stop him from cashing in his "season ticket" for a "one way ride." One night, at thirty-three years of age, Scott passed out from an alcohol/drug overdose. When they found him the next morning, Bon Scott's arrogantly bold affront to God had been literally fulfilled.

Angus Young (lead guitarist) and the other members regrouped, found a new singer in Brian Johnson, and hit the road again declaring, "We're Back in Black." "Hells Bells," a hit off of that album, showed no signs of sobered repentance. Johnson seemed to be a "reincarnation" of Scott, singing about giving "black sensations" up one's spine. "If you're into evil," he challenged, you are most certainly "a friend of mine." As a clincher he pointed out that if good could be found on the left, he'd definitely be "stickin' to the right."

AC/DC's hell-raising music has been called "infantile" by critics, but loyal fans (mostly male) could care less, believing in the band because they know AC/DC's on-stage persona isn't an act. Explaining their song "The Jack" (a British term for gonorrhea), Bon Scott once told an interviewer, "We were living in this household of very friendly ladies and everyone got the jack. So we wrote this song."[1] One pro-rock journal commenting on Scott's death was even forced to acknowledge, "Throughout the AC/DC catalogue there is a disturbing correlation between pleasure/sex/drunkenness and unconsciousness/death which has now reached its tragic culmination."[2]

Their approach may seem moronic and barbaric, but those who buy their albums can at least attest to the fact that there is no hype in the way the band sings and lives. "If You Want Blood (You've Got It)," an early album, shows AC/DC's guitarist impaled on the neck of a guitar, lying on the floor, and drenched in blood. This writer once asked a rock musician who does cover versions of AC/DC songs to comment on the significance of this depiction. "Rock and roll kills," he calmly replied with all seriousness. It did kill Bon Scott. The haunting question is, "Who's next?"

[1] *Circus*, January 30, 1980, p. 34.
[2] *Ibid.*, p. 35.

BENATAR, PAT

"Hit Me with Your Best Shot," Pat Benatar invites with sado-masochistic sauciness. It's hardly the challenge one expects from a diminutive, 90-pound rock/sex-kitten. Offstage she admits to a nondrug, domesticated life-style. In concert, her stage presence is sassy and brazen, as she struts about in her "glued-on" spandex suit. Songs like "Fire and Ice" and "Take It Anyway You Want It," enhance her sexist image of striking back rather than limping away brokenhearted. Whether her raunchiness is real or contrived matters little to the males in her audience. They see her parody of female machismo as being perversely alluring. Concerned that her record company once produced an ad in which they airbrushed away part of her leotard top to make her appear naked, Pat commented, "If that is gonna sell records, then it's a real sorry thing."[1]

[1] *Rolling Stone*, October 16, 1980, p. 13.

BLACK SABBATH

Just when rock critics thought that Punk and New Wave had
buried heavy-metal, Black Sabbath came back from the "dead" to
baptize audiences with their downer-depressive sounds. With
Ozzy Osbourne gone from the group, new singer Ronnie James
Dio kept up the demonic overtones by flashing the audience an
"11 Cornuto" (Sicilian for "The Horn") sign.[1] With his fist thrust
into the air (index and pinky finger extended), Dio's exhibition
of the devil's salute used by black magic practitioners only serves
to reinforce the image held by those who still see Sabbath as
rock's foremost satanic symbol. Even more unsettling is Dio's
invitation asking audiences to mimic the sign and direct their
attention to an onstage cross which abruptly bursts into flames.[2]
Dio declares that his new role as head vocalist has maintained
the group's sense of "mysticism and doom."[3] Sabbath has made
some efforts to tone down their occult image but not enough
to disillusion die-hard fans, who are described by one rock
magazine as the kind who ". . . get wasted, mindless, and let a
black menacing wave cross over them for the evening."[4]

When someone stole a special guitar owned by Tony Iommi
(the "axe" had thirteen crosses inlaid on the fretboard), fellow
bandmember Geezer Butler put a hex on the unfortunate
criminal. The guitar had been previously stolen but quickly
returned by a repentant thief who confessed that unending misery
and tragedy had been his lot while he had the guitar in his hands.[5]
Might the same be said for Black Sabbath fans who cherish their
albums? Sabbath's album "Heaven and Hell" could well be seen
as a choice instead of a religious commentary.

[1]*Circus*, August 26, 1980, p. 22.
[2]*Billboard*, November 1, 1980, p. 34.
[3]*Rolling Stone*, May 15, 1980, p. 34.
[4]*Circus*, March 31, 1981, p. 30.
[5]*The Vancouver Sun*, August 22, 1980.

BLONDIE

Blondie may be the name for a six-member pop/New Wave
band, but to millions of American males, ex-Playboy Bunny
Deborah Harry is the sexual and musical essence of the group.
"I've always thought the main ingredients in rock are sex and

sass," Debbie declares.[1] Her fans don't argue as she lyrically
invites lovers to "roll her" in "designer sheets" because she
can never "get enough . . ." (from "Call Me"). Her live-in
lover/manager Chris Stein calmly adds, "Everybody takes it for
granted that rock and roll is synonymous with sex."[2] Debbie, a
former heroin addict, is rock's blonde (dyed) bombshell, complete
with dark roots, smeared makeup, and outdated miniskirts,
looking like an Andy Warhol movie extra. Newsweek magazine
surveyed her appeal and concluded it was based on an "abstracted
erotocism" with lyrical "anthems of narcissism."[3] Another
periodical commented that Harry's punk style of lost innocence
reflected only "absurdism and nihilism."[4] Her solo album "Koo
Koo" featured oversized acupuncture needles piercing her neck
and head. With jeans commercials to her credit and movie offers
in the making, acceptance by the establishment lies just around
the corner. It remains to be seen how this will affect her mock
seriousness reflected in tunes like "Die Young Stay Pretty," and
her admiration for her platinum heroines, Marilyn Monroe and
Jayne Mansfield. They did just that.

[1]Hit Parader, September 1979, p. 31.
[2]People, May 21, 1979.
[3]Newsweek, August 24, 1981, p. 77.
[4]Vogue, July 1980, p. 186.

BLUE OYSTER CULT

"This long Island quintet continues to be to pop music what the
Ouija board is to parlor games."[1] So said one rock reviewer.
Describing the demonic character of this grinding, heavy-metal
music, lead singer Eric Bloom says, "It's got to be not oppressive,
but felt!" But their potent hard-rock sounds are the least of
worries. BOC lyrics describe death in its "Sunday best" and
implore listeners, "Don't Turn Your Back" on "intuition" and
"superstition." Their album "Fire of Unknown Origin" dispelled
any doubts about the intent of their songs with titles like "Veteran
of Psychic Wars" and "Vengeance (The Pact)." (The latter comes
complete with a laughing voice as an arrow is thrust through the
head of a nameless person.) On "After Dark" the group apparently
proclaims its devotion to the devil by addressing an unnamed
essence whose voice calls from "far away." The singer responds
because he has "no choice" after "terror took control." He goes

on to extol the satanic virtues of darkness and concludes that this affinity has brought him "true salvation," with "power" as the ultimate "drug" he has been seeking. The echoed scream finishing the song will undoubtedly warm the hearts of committed BOC fans even as it chills the spine of Christians who have no trouble identifying the source of this "power."

[1]*People*, September 14, 1981.

FLEETWOOD MAC

Before each concert, the backstage dressing rooms of Fleetwood Mac members must be stocked with spareribs, fresh limes, white wine (Blue Nun), cognac, and two bottles of Don Perignon.[1] Their contracts demand such treatment as one of the perks of rock power. "You can go your own way," they once declared to Mac fans, and each individual in the group has done just that—bass guitarist John McVie to a drug bust in his Napili Hawaiian paradise home; Mick Fleetwood to Ghana, Africa, to record budding native musicians; and Stevie Nicks into accentuated exploration of the occult.

Stevie (previously discussed on page 42) admits to believing in spirits, confesses that Halloween is her favorite night of the year, dabbles in reincarnation philosophy, wants to talk to a ghost, and expresses a desire to build her own pyramid and live in a witch-house. The idea for the cover of her solo album "Bella Donna" came to her in a dream. It features a crystal ball (endorsing divination), a tambourine (symbolizing the porthole of perception to the spirit world), and three roses (representing the power of pyramids).[2]

"Bella Donna" album credits list Maya Design studios for clothing assistance. (Maya is a name for the Hindu goddess *Devi*, who represents the illusory nature of the material world.) Bella Donna is also the name for a powerful poison, an interesting choice of words for an album title which may inherently forewarn of its toxic content. As Stevie (who wrote the lyrics) declares in the title cut, "Bella Donna... sort of captures your soul."[3] Is it any wonder that *Rolling Stone* magazine calls her "Fleetwood Mac's blond priestess of the occult?"[4]

[1]*The Vancouver Sun*, December 27, 1979, p. 6.
[2]*Rolling Stone*, September 3, 1981, p. 18.

³Lyric sheet for "Bella Donna."
⁴*Rolling Stone*, September 17, 1981, p. 57.

JOURNEY

People magazine called them a band with an affinity for "marijuana and loud, suggestive songs."[1] Their own manager, Herbie Herbert, confessed that Journey fans generally show up at concerts with "a pill and a joint."[2] Their drug sentiments have been underscored with substantial contributions directed to NORMAL (The National Organization for Reform of Marijuana Laws), America's most vocal pro-pot lobby. "Who's Crying Now," their chart-topping single, might well rhetorically be answered, "The parents of children who may find marijuana more accessible due to Journey's endorsements." Record buyers have a clear moral choice before them, knowing the destination of part of Journey's proceeds.

¹*People*, October 12, 1981.
²*Rolling Stone*, November 12, 1981, p. 56.

JUDAS PRIEST

With a stage act ranging from smoke bombs to bullwhips, the bellicose, leather-clad image of Judas Priest fits well with their heavy-metal ear-splitting music. "We wear what goes with the music," declares guitarist Glenn Tipton.[1] Dressed in chains and studs, singer Rob Halford has been known to drop his leather drawers mid-concert. "If you're not the type of person this music can reach, then there's nothing more you can do about it. It's just a whole experience of something that happens inside of you."[2] When asked if he was personally involved in the S & M (sado-masochism) love torture-techniques parodied in his performances, Halford replied, "To a certain extent. Sexually I have always been to the fullest extent of the experience that S & M has to offer. It's nice to experiment by yourself and get off on whatever you get off on."[3] A rock magazine ad promoting one of their albums may have said it best, "Judas Priest has sin for sale."

¹*Billboard*, July 5, 1980, p. 28.
²*Circus*, July 22, 1980, p. 30.
³*Rolling Stone*, September 15, 1980, p. 14.

KISS

"We're the cultural heroes of our day,"[1] Gene Simmons declared, but it was bound to end sometime. First, "the Cat," drummer Peter Criss, split with the group and went solo. Then record sales tapered off. They had already sold $60 million worth and amassed a value (according to an accountant's balance sheet) putting them ahead of 1500 corporations on the New York Stock Exchange. Their paeans to pagan pubescence had astonished and revolted audiences all over the world. (". . . cycles and whips, just all the things little girls dream about," Simmons boasted of their sadomasochistic images.)[2]

KISS had smoke-bombed their way into the seventies. By the early eighties it looked like the breezy ballads of Christopher Cross and the conservative wave of Ronald Reagan had done them in. When this book reaches the reader's hands, KISS may be disbanded, in limbo, or surging ahead bigger than ever. This writer's obituary notice of KISS may be premature, but the jaded public seems (at the writing of this update) ready for fresh faces they can actually see.

[1]*People*, August 18, 1980, p. 100.
[2]*Rock*, November 1976, p. 42.

LED ZEPPELIN

One of the world's longest reigning rock bands finally met its demise in late 1980. A series of tragedies had bedeviled the group: lead singer Robert Plant was seriously injured in an automobile crash; Plant's son died from an unknown illness; a Zeppelin roadie also died mysteriously; and drummer John "Bonzo" Bonham was found dead on September 24, 1980. Bonham's death was attributed officially to the ingestion of "forty measures" of vodka. Traces of Motival (a drug used to curb anxiety) were also found in his blood.[1]

Bonham died in the home of Jimmy Page, fueling rumors of sinister overtones resulting from Page's fascination with black magic. John had once declared, "I'd like to play for another 20 years . . . I just can't see it happening . . . it's a foreboding—vultures."[2]

Most observers attributed the band's break-up to Page's satanic obsession and his veneration for occultist Aleister Crowley, whom he called "an unrecognized genius of twentieth century thinking."[3] Bonham was known as rock and roll's "bad guy" for his reputation as a hotel room destroyer. Perhaps Bonham, known to associates as "the Beast," met his match that September evening in Crowley's former estate (Page's home). The residence is said to be haunted by a death curse. Ironically, it was Crowley who had officially renamed himself, "The Beast—666."

[1]*Rolling Stone*, November 13, 1980, p. 22.
[2]*Circus*, November 30, 1980, p. 20.
[3]*Ibid*.

OZZY OSBOURNE

With a decade of service to Black Sabbath behind him, Ozzy Osbourne, the diabolical former lead singer for England's heavy-metal Satan-rockers, is on his own. Lest anyone think that his split with Sabbath is for the better, Ozzy warns, "I'm just as evil and just as crazy as ever."[1]

No one who was there the day he bit the head off a live dove at a CBS executive meeting would doubt his claim. "I wanted them to remember me," he explains, describing how he spat the remains on the table.[2] There's a lot to remember about Ozzy. Though he acknowledges the Satan-worshiping image in Sabbath's early days was a marketing ploy, he never retreats from his own fascination with Lucifer. He professes a belief in future and past existences, one of which was lived as a "servant of the devil."[3] He also remains devoted to Aleister Crowley, the famous British spiritualist (see the section on Led Zeppelin, p. 134), "a phenomenon of his time," says Ozzy.[4]

Drugs seem to have been as much a part of his life as has been the devil. He admits to taking LSD every day for years, spending $1000 a week on dope, snorting cocaine "by the bagful," and sampling heroin.[5] Though personally opposed to hard drug usage, he qualifies his abstention by adding, "I can't say that I knock drugs. When you're having fun it's great, but when someone has to pay for it, it is bad."[6]

His release "Diary of a Madman" was promoted by a $2 million concert tour featuring macabre props and special effects including gallons of pigs' blood.[7] A printed release enclosed with the LP shared Ozzy's feelings: "I have become infatuated with the

feeling of horror. . . . If my ideas seem disordered in intellect or
slightly psychotic . . . it is because they are." Ozzy once thought
he wanted to build a black cathedral behind his house, but in
spite of such demonic collusion he argues somewhat unconvincingly, "I am not a bad person . . . or wish harm on anyone."[8]

[1]*Hit Parader*, March 1981, p. 27.
[2]*Rolling Stone*, May 14, 1981, p. 41.
[3]*Circus*, August 26, 1980, p. 26.
[4]*Ibid.*
[5]*People*, September 7, 1981.
[6]*Circus*, June 30, 1981, p. 39.
[7]*Rolling Stone*, November 12, 1981, p. 39.
[8]*Circus*, August 26, 1980, p. 26.

PINK FLOYD

With forty-foot-high helium-inflated pigs floating in the air, a
fussilade of fireworks, the amplified sounds of someone walking
on the ceiling, or a 35 by 210-foot cardboard wall rising from the
stage, a Pink Floyd concert is rock theater at its best (or worst,
depending on one's moral perspective). Their *avant-garde*
sounds, propelled by the sale of 6½ million units of their 1973
release "Dark Side of the Moon," blitz drug-doped audiences
with space-rock sounds that a high-tech buff would love.

This British group had its genesis in the sixties under the
tutelage of the acid-experimenting "genius" Syd Barrett. His
psychedelic inclinations introduced the group to sight and sound
effects that would accompany tunes like "Chapter 24" (a musical
adaptation of the occultic *I Ching*). Barrett, who quit the group,
has long since been left behind for the Pinkies' space-rock voyage
of the eighties.

One album, "The Wall," earned Pink Floyd an amazing $20
million in one year by topping the charts for weeks on end. "The
Wall" chronicles the emotional torment of a successful rock
star (a.k.a. Roger Waters, who wrote most of the lyrics and music)
who builds up a "wall" of defenses against an absent father,
smothering mother, and sadistic schoolmaster.

"The Wall" lyrics explore psychic powers ("Nobody Home"),
sex ("Young Lust"—"I need a dirty woman"), and educational
anarchism. In the title song, Pink Floyd caustically intones that
youth "don't need no education" or "thought control." What high

school teacher could cope with students who had heeded the Wall's plea: "Leave them kids alone!"

PLASMATICS

If smashing television sets, battering Cadillacs with a sledge-hammer, and blowing up concert stages stacked with musical equipment is your bag, you'll love the Plasmatics. Lead guitarist, 6-foot 5-inch Richie Stotts (who sports a blue-dyed Mohawk haircut), bloodies himself by banging his head against his guitar. Wendy O. Williams, a veteran performer on the Times Square live-sex circuit, appears scantily clad (often topless) with electrical tape or shaving cream strategically placed to avoid vice squad raids. Before wrecking amps and guitars with her trusty sledgehammer, Wendy uses it to masturbate publicly, an act which has earned her arrests in Cleveland and Milwaukee. Of her destructive and erotic exhibitionism, Wendy declares, "We have to do it. I have all this violence inside of me that I have to get out."[1] With Punk music that sounds like Black Sabbath on amphetamines and a stage act that rivals *Hustler* for depravity, the Plasmatics' album "New Hope for the Wretched" heralds a titled optimism that seems only half true.

[1]*Rocky Mountain News*, (A.P. story), February 13, 1981, p. 41 c.

THE PRETENDERS

Leather-love songs of violent amatory experiences might be expected from the likes of Judas Priest and Scorpion, but Chrissie Hynde of the Pretenders is, after all, a woman. That doesn't seem to hold her back. In "Tattooed Love Boys" she describes a quasi-rape scene in which her lover treats her so roughly that a plastic surgeon is required to patch things up. Sex to Chrissie may mean that lust not only "turns to anger" but also transforms "a kiss to a slug." "Up the Neck" records her emotions after one such encounter and "Bad Boys Get Spanked" turns the tables, complete with a periodic whacking sound accompanied by groans and screams. "Brass in Pocket" explains her plans to vary the normal procedures of love-making by inventively using her "imagination" as well as her "arms... legs... fingers... style."

With ripped jeans, crinkled leather jacket, and disheveled hair, Chrissie evokes the consummate punk gang look. Toughness, not femininity, is her forte. "Every night I get some girl coming backstage who says to me that halfway through the set they forgot I was a girl," Ms. Hynde brags![1] Her coaxing vulgarity and profane street language accompany a cultivated interest in palmistry, numerology, and black magic. The boys in the band also reflect her wayward ways. Guitarist James Honeyman-Scott acknowledges a former addiction to speed, acute cirrhosis of the liver from alcohol, and a proclivity for cocaine.[2] Her romance with the Kinks' Ray Davies and her growing popularity have enabled Chrissie to tone down her image ever-so-slightly. The shaggy look of her sheepdog hairdo has been lightly coiffured and her morbid black eyeliner has been softened with feminine shades of pink. Chrissie's song, "I'm the Adulteress" was direct to the point. Davies' second wife sued for divorce on grounds of adultery, naming Ms. Hynde as co-respondent. "I love pretending," Chrissie admits in one song lyric. Too bad she doesn't mean it.

[1]*Circus*, October 31, 1981, p. 25.
[2]*Rolling Stone*, May 20, 1980, p. 29.

QUEEN

From their crest, which depicts animals representing the astrological signs of each member, to their tours, which are rock's most lavish and expensive, Queen spares nothing to maintain its image as one of the most outlandish acts in the music business. Their tours have also featured snake charmers, strippers, transvestites, and a naked lady who smokes cigarettes between her legs! Though Freddie mercury (the band's lead singer) maintains the most debaucherous public image, he is rivaled by fellow member Roger Taylor. Taylor admits, "I like strippers and wild parties with naked women. I'd love to own a whorehouse. What a wonderful way to make a living."[1]

[1]*Rolling Stone*, June 11, 1981, p. 46.

THE ROLLING STONES

He once declared he'd rather be dead than sing "Satisfaction" when he'd be 30. As he and the other Stones continue to rock on (their 1981 tour grossed an estimated $127 million, including

$300,000 a day on T-shirts sales alone), Mick Jagger has revised the dreaded age of demise to 40. Jagger, who has divorced Bianca for the promiscuous charms of model Jerry Hall, has certainly not gained any moral maturity with age. His sadomasochistic view of women lingers on with salacious lines like, "When the whip comes down," and "Am I rough enough?" (from "Beast of Burden").

Simple sex hasn't been totally abandoned. "Emotional Rescue" found Jagger lamenting that he was hot for a girl who was "so cold" that she had an "Arctic soul." Sneeringly he warned her when she got old nobody would care that she had been a "sweet, sweet virgin." "Tattoo You" continued in the Stones sexist tradition with tunes like "Little T & A" and "Start Me" (Jagger complains about his lover's violent love-making manners of "roughing it up" by commenting, "You make a grown man cry").

Jagger's Luciferian personification has been lately rivaled by guitarist Keith Richard. Richard's heroin drug bust highlighted a habit he'd had for ten years. Former associate Tony Sanchez charged in a book entitled *Up and Down with the Rolling Stones* that for a 1975 tour Richard underwent a total blood-exchange transfusion to get past U. S. Immigration officials. Sanchez also accuses Richard and his common-law wife, Anita Pallenberg, with sojourns into black magic, bisexuality, and turning children on to heroin and cocaine.[1] *Up and Down* also claims that Richard's drug habit ran to $1000 a day. In Tony's words, the Stones are "the loneliest men I have ever known."[2]

For his part, Richard (now supposedly clean of smack and split from Pallenberg for model Patti Hansen) seems unashamed of his flirtation with addictive drugs. "I don't regret what I did," he says. "Everybody needs a little kick from something. . . ."[3] Mick Jagger adds his qualified endorsement of cocaine by declaring, "If you want to take it, fine . . . what a boring drug."[4]

The adulation with which the Stones are worshiped borders on the messianic. Jagger does nothing to dispel the image, singing in "Emotional Rescue" that he wants to be "your saviour . . . steadfast and true." However, *Newsweek* magazine was more correct to the point, calling the Stones' music for the eighties an "erotic exorcism for a doomed decade."[5]

[1]*Newsweek*, September 17, 1979, p. 95.
[2]*Circus*, December 11, 1979, p. 35.
[3]*US*, November 10, 1981, p. 29.

158   ROCK

⁴*Rolling Stone*, May 29, 1980, p. 34.
⁵*Newsweek*, October 5, 1981, p. 61.

SPRINGSTEEN, BRUCE

He has been compared to Elvis, Dylan, and Jagger. When his
album "Born to Run" hit the charts in the mid-seventies,
Newsweek and *Time* proclaimed him the new-and-future superstar. His fall from the top was quick, but he reemerged three
years later, rocking until he became one of the biggest concert
draws on the East Coast. With the help of the E Street Band he
puts on one of the most emotional and exhilarating shows ever
witnessed in rock and roll. Springsteen leaps onto amps, tumbles
into crowds, and vocalizes with frenetic abandon up to four hours
a night. The hard edge to his music evokes images of the cars,
bikes, and concrete scenes so much a part of his native New
Jersey. His lyrical allusions to sex square more with the traditional
street-level macho solicitations than the androgynous intimations
of a Mick Jagger or Freddie Mercury. Love is summed up in a
casual reference to Mary, a girl he got pregnant ("Thunder
Road"), and the lust of life is epitomized by the "stolen car" he
drives down Elridge Avenue (from "The River" album). The
spiritual emptiness of Springsteen's Asbury wasteland is
symbolized by his lament, "When I was growing up the only
thing that never let me down was rock and roll."[1] As one secular
rock critic put it, "Upon this rock (the statement just quoted)
Springsteen has built his church. . . ."[2]

[1]*Time*, August 7, 1978, p. 73.
[2]*Ibid.*

STYX

"There's something in a name," says the old maxim. In Styx's
case, it could be true. Styx is the sacred river that encircled Hades
in Greek mythology. Such metaphysical inclinations perhaps
portend some significance, though this Windy City quintet insists
the name was chosen only as "one of the hundreds" they tried.[1]
One rock periodical wondered at their "sorcerer-like appeal to
fans' imagination," leading another rock insider to call their
popularity "the Second Coming of God."[2] Beautiful ballads like
"Lady" and "Babe" mix with mystical allusions to gypsy queens

and crystal balls. More talented and less offensive than some bands, their nominal designation can give little comfort to the Christian teenager who ought to view hell as the place of the damned, hardly a title to be emblazoned on T-shirts and album jackets.

[1]*Circus*, December 11, 1979, p. 23.
[2]*Ibid.*

VAN HALEN

When a rock band is self-described as "a group of barbarians who are sweeping around the world," it's obvious their goals transcend mere musical performances.[1] Lead singer David Lee Roth confesses, "I've managed to live out 100 percent of my fantasies with pretty women I've met on the road."[2] Phallically gesturing with the microphone postured erectly between his legs he adds, "We celebrate all the sex and violence of television. . . . That's Van Halen."[3]

Roth is only one-fourth of the group, which includes bass guitarist Michael Anthony and the Dutch-born Van Halen brothers, Edward and Alex. Edward declares, "I'm in rock and roll because I don't like being told what to do."[4] But Roth's high-leaping, crotch-thrusting antics define the group's philosophy more definitively. With autoerotic abandon he proclaims, ". . . whatever your vice, whatever your sexual ideas . . . whatever somebody else can't do in his nine-to-five job, I can do in rock and roll . . . I'm in the job to exercise my sexual fantasies. When I'm onstage it's like doing it with 20,000 of your closest friends . . . I'm proud of the way we live. . . ."[5]

The hedonistic sensuality Roth encourages has led him to suggest that Lloyds of London offer paternity insurance for rock stars.[6] With tunes like "Feel Your Love Tonight," "Running with the Devil," "Everybody Wants Some," and "I'm Your Ice Cream Man" ("My flavor's guaranteed to satisfy") to their credit, Van Halen probably needs it. At least they give fair warning before assaulting their audience with debauchery and decibels. "Women and Children First," says one of their album titles.

[1]*Circus*, October 10, 1978, p. 26.
[2]*Ibid.*, November 14, 1979, p. 42.
[3]*Ibid.*, October 17, 1978, p. 39.
[4]*Ibid.*, May 13, 1980, p. 23.

5*Rolling Stone*, September 4, 1980, pp. 9-10, 21.
6*People*, October 17, 1981, p. 12.

THE WHO

The body count is in, and here are the results: Three Mile Island, Diablo Canyon, and all nuclear facilities combined—0; The Who—11. So why aren't placard-bearing protesters picketing Who concerts? After all, it was Peter Townshend himself who declared in a moment of rare remorse after that fateful Cincinnati concert, "You try to convince yourself that it had nothing to do with us, but that would be a bit childish. . . . We're a big part of rock and roll so we feel partly responsible."[1]

One rock magazine commented on the tragic death of eleven Who fans, trampled under the feet of their compatriots who in their dope-induced hysteria were rushing to be first at the foot of the stage: "Who's going to see The Who? Not Boy Scouts. Rock mega-stars must wake up. They hold sway over an entire generation . . . there is very definitely a responsibility that goes with it."[2]

Keith Moon's death and the Cincinnati debacle have done little to sober Townshend and Co. Peter declared to the press, "We had to reduce it because if we'd actually admitted to ourselves the true significance of the event [Cincinnati] . . . we could not have gone on. . . . We don't [expletive] around worrying about eleven people dying. . . . When you go on the road you put an armour around yourself . . . you almost go into a trance."[3]

Violence isn't the only message of The Who. An album entitled "Face Dances" vividly describes the compulsion of masturbatory impulses while asking, "How can you do it alone?" In "You" the lyricist describes his lover as inviting his advances with open arms while her "legs are crossed."

While The Who continues to live on the outer limits of rock's sanity, Townshend confesses, "Rock is going to kill me somehow. It gets everybody in the end."[4] Perhaps the destructive message they deliver is best illustrated by post-Cincinnati T-shirts, stamped with footprints and reading, "I survived The Who concert."

1*Billboard*, December 22, 1979, p. 41.
2*Circus*, January 22, 1980, p. 54.
3*Rolling Stone*, June 26, 1980, p. 38.
4*Time*, December 17, 1979, p. 94.